Common Sense Matters

Thoughts On Life, On Leading, On Selling

Eric Levine

Copyright © 2014 Eric Levine
All rights reserved.

ISBN: 149972313X
ISBN 13: 9781499723137

Dedicated to my Grandchildren who never cease to amaze me.
Chelsea
Madison
Zachary
Joshua
Shayna
Cassidy
Kyle

COMMON SENSE MATTERS

Prologue... vii

Twenty years from now you will be more disappointed by the things you didn't do than by the ones you did. So, throw off the bowlines. Sail away from the safe harbor. Catch the trade winds in your sails. Explore. Dream. Discover.
Mark Twain, Author

On Life... 1

Old age is like everything else. To make a success of it you have to start young.
Fred Astaire, Dancer

On Leading... 107

If you are going through hell, keep going.
Sir Winston Churchill, British Prime Minister

On Selling... 195

"Timid salesmen have skinny kids."
Zig Ziglar, Motivational Speaker

PROLOGUE

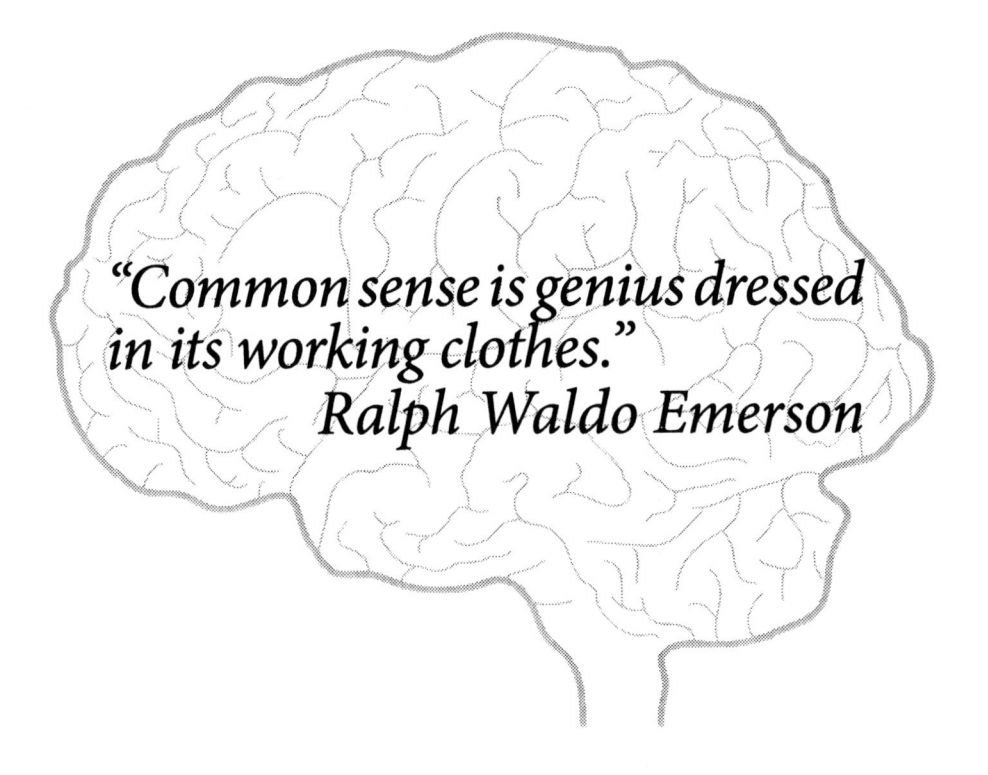

"Common sense is genius dressed in its working clothes."
Ralph Waldo Emerson

COMMON SENSE MATTERS

I put pen to paper to share some of my thoughts on common sense…

My grandchildren and friends have, from time to time, asked me to share some of my experiences and tidbits of what I have learned over my many years in business—and interfacing with so many different interesting people. Considering I am getting a little long in the tooth, I thought now might be a good time to do this. Time has a way of moving quickly and catching you unaware of the passing years. It seems like it was only yesterday that I was young and newly married and embarking on a new life with my wife, Bebe. Yet, in a way, it seems like eons ago, and I wonder where all those years went. I cannot believe we are married over fifty- four years. I know that I lived them all. I have periodic glimpses of how it was back then and of all my hopes and dreams.

But, here it is…the winter of my life, and it catches me by surprise. How did I get here so fast? Where did the years and my youth go? I remember well seeing older people through the years and thinking that those older people were years away from me and that winter was so far off that I could not imagine what it would be like.

And now, my friends are retired and getting gray. They move slower, and I see older people now. Some are in better, and some are in worse, shape than me, but I see the great change. Like me, their age is beginning to show, and we are now those older people that we used to see, and never thought we would be. Some days I now find that getting out

Prologue

of bed is a target. And taking a nap is no longer a treat; it is mandatory. For if I don't, of my own free will, I will simply fall asleep where I sit.

I now enter into this new season of my life unprepared for all the aches and pains and the loss of the ability and strength to do the things I wish I had done but never did. But, though the winter has come—and I am not sure how long it will last—this I know: when my time is over on Earth, I have the faith that a new adventure will begin.

Yes, I have regrets. There are things I wish I hadn't done…and things I should have. It is all in a lifetime.

So, my children, my grandchildren, my friends, and anyone that may read these words I share, let me remind you that your winter will be here faster than you think. Whatever you would like to accomplish in your life, please do it quickly! Don't put things off too long; life goes by so fast. Do what you can today because no one knows what season of life they are in. Live for today and say the things you want your loved ones to remember. And hope that they love you for all you have done for them in their lives (and forgive you for all the things they may have wanted you to do—which you never did).

I sincerely hope that some of what I share with you in the following pages may help make you successful—whatever you consider success to be.

I know you do not spell success c-a-s-h or m-o-n-e-y. Not that money isn't, in some instances, an important yardstick of success. For most people, true happiness and success have very little to do with money. It has to do with family; it has to do with relationships; it has to do with how we treat others; it has to do with honesty and integrity; and it has to do with how we feel about ourselves. Do we really like who we are? Do we respect ourselves? Because if we don't have these elements in our lives, true happiness and success will be an elusive dream. To this end, I want to share with you some of what I have learned and experienced over the sixty-plus years' experience I have had in business. I have travelled on what I believe is a simple journey of success.

In this book, I will touch on three subjects: Life. Leadership. Selling.

<u>Life</u> is every moment we deal with, 24/7. Good, bad, or indifferent, it is there when we wake in the morning and when we go to sleep at night. It is how we handle each moment in time.

<u>Leadership</u> touches nearly everyone. Ninety percent of people either follow a leader or are leaders themselves. In our family, at work, in our faith community, in our neighborhood, there are leaders at all levels—and true leaders are not always at the top.

Then you have that 10 percent who want to be an island, and that's OK too.

<u>Selling.</u> I believe nothing happens until a sale is made. The serpent did a sales job on Adam and Eve, making selling the real "oldest profession in the world." I do not mean to minimize the importance of any job or profession by saying this, BUT…if we never had doctors, life would still go on (only the average life span would be forty-five instead of ninety). If we never had attorneys, disputes would still be resolved (but there would be a few more black eyes). Even if a person is applying for a job, they need to sell themselves. It may be a server "selling" you the idea of ordering the special of the day or a stock broker selling you on the idea of purchasing certain stocks. Or you may be selling your partner

PROLOGUE

on the idea it's time to go home. But we are always selling an idea or product—or buying one.

If you buy a pencil, try to calculate how many salespeople were involved, from the selling of the tree from which it was made, to the time you hold it in your hand. You will see the number exceeds ten. For this reason, I believe everyone needs a certain skill level in selling to maximize their potential in this world. Some people may choose to call it marketing, cajoling, influencing, persuading, bartering, or coaxing. But as William Shakespeare said in Romeo and Juliet, "A rose by any other name will smell as sweet." It is all selling. If no one sold anything to anyone, the world would come to a standstill.

I hope you can pick up a few "gems" for yourself in this book; perhaps it may teach you something, or simply bring a smile to your lips.

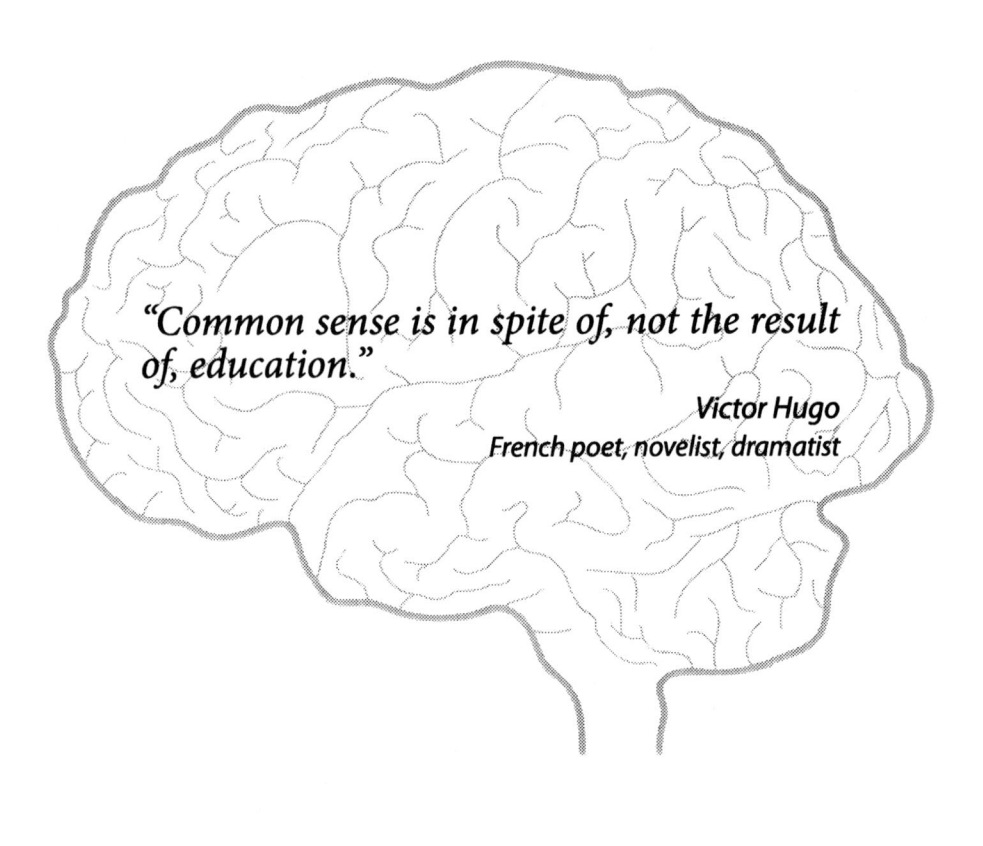

"Common sense is in spite of, not the result of, education."

Victor Hugo
French poet, novelist, dramatist

COMMON SENSE MATTERS

You may wonder why the phrase "common sense" is so meaningful to me. I think it is because I have met so many highly successful people in my life, from a financial point of view, from a personal achievement point of view, from a family /relationship point of view, and from a community service point of view, who really never had much of an education at all, but were endowed with common sense. It was not the fact that they only had a high school education as opposed to a college degree that made them successful; it had little to do with their education and a whole lot to do with good, old-fashioned common sense. Education does not necessarily equal common sense! Please understand I am not knocking higher education, because I truly believe an education is essential in today's world. But education skills can be learned, whereas common sense is a natural instinct, one that is "caught," not "taught."

Please don't interpret this incorrectly. I am NOT saying a great education is the wrong thing. In fact, exactly the opposite. But what I am saying is that without common sense, one's potential in life is hindered and limited, irrespective of one's education.

Finally...
As I finished penning these few common sense thoughts, I was looking for one word to encapsulate what differentiates successful personalities from unsuccessful personalities. After many arguments with myself, I settled on the word "Attitude." I feel that warrants an explanation—and try as I might, I could not come up with a single experience or story that

explained what I felt in my soul. I did, however, come across a parable, by an unknown author, which hit the nail right on the head:

There once was a woman who woke up one morning, looked in the mirror, and noticed she only had three hairs on her head.
"Well," she said, "I think I'll braid my hair today. So she did, and she had a wonderful day.

The next day, she woke up, looked in the mirror, and saw she only had two hairs on her head.
"Hmmm," she said, "I think I'll part my hair down the middle today."

So she did, and she had a grand day.

The next day, she woke up, looked in the mirror, and noticed she only had one hair on her head.
"Well," she said, "today I'm going to wear my hair in a ponytail." And she did. And she had a fun, fun day.

The next day, she woke up and noticed she had not a single hair on her head.
"YEAH!" she exclaimed. "I don't have to fix my hair today."

Thank you for sharing some of my thoughts about life, leadership, and selling, and I do hope you have some "AHA!!" moments that may enrich your life.

Common Sense Matters

The *Investor's Business Daily* has spent years analyzing leaders and successful people in all walks of life. Most have ten traits that, when combined, can turn dreams into reality. They publish these traits every day in their newspaper. I would like to share them with you before I get into the essence of the pages that follow, as I believe they are truly Words of Wisdom—real **Common Sense**.

1. **How you think is everything.** Always be positive. Think success, not failure. Avoid a negative environment.
2. **Decide on your true dreams and goals.** Write down your specific goals and develop a plan to reach them.
3. **Take action.** Goals are nothing without action. Don't be afraid to get started. Just do it.
4. **Never stop learning.** Go back to school. Read books. Get training and acquire skills.
5. **Be persistent and work hard.** Success is a marathon, not a sprint. Never give up.
6. **Learn to analyze details.** Get all the facts, all the input. Learn from your mistakes.
7. **Focus your time and money.** Don't let other people or things distract you.
8. **Don't be afraid to innovate, be different.** Following the herd is a sure way to mediocrity.
9. **Deal and communicate with people effectively.** No person is an island. Learn to understand and motivate others.
10. **Be honest and dependable; take responsibility.** Otherwise the other nine won't matter.

Investors Business Daily.com

COMMON SENSE MATTERS

ON LIFE

"Life is what happens when you are busy making other plans."
                                    John Lennon

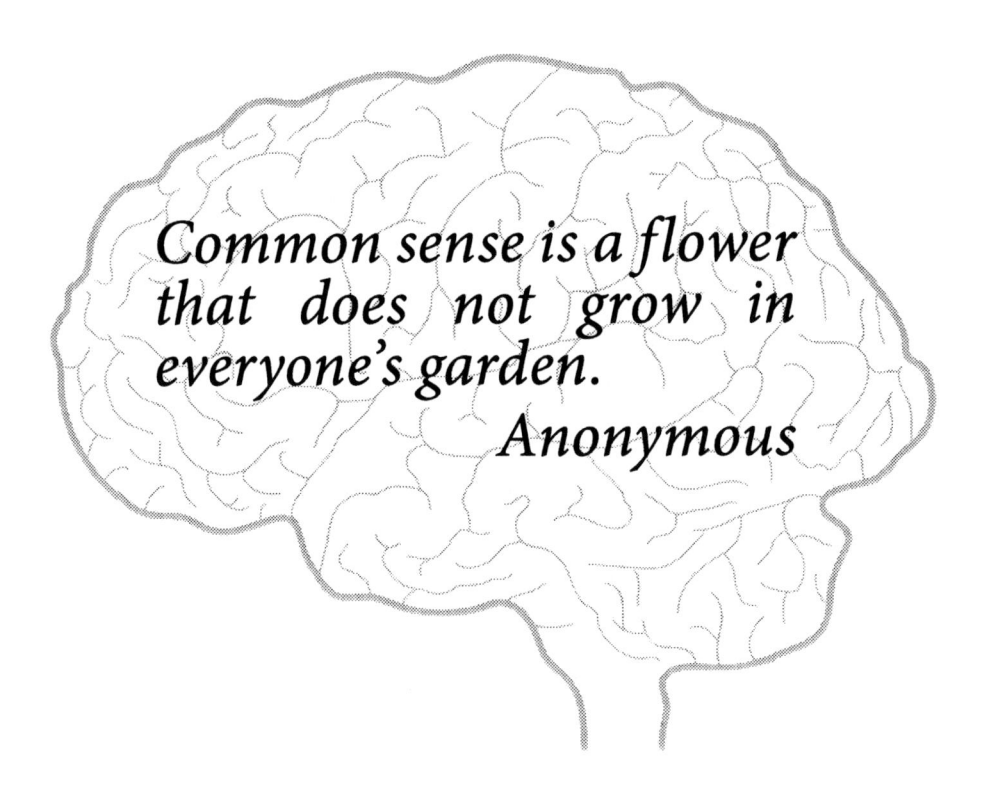

Common sense is a flower that does not grow in everyone's garden.
     Anonymous

COMMON SENSE MATTERS

A Common Sense Observation on Life

Life is a journey through which we all travel. Some of us make the best of the trip, irrespective of the problems and challenges we encounter; others have challenges that they find difficult to handle.

By and large, however, most people are always striving to make the best of the hand they have been dealt in life, regardless of the peaks and valleys they encounter. We see this all the time with motivational sayings; we see it in people's homes; and we see it in people's offices. How do we turn life's lemons into lemonade?

I believe all the beautiful motivational sayings we see and books we read are wonderful to create the climate in which self-motivation takes place. But in the end, that's all it is, a climate or an ambiance.

True motivation must come from within. True happiness must come from within. The setting of your life's values must come from within. In short, your journey through life starts with you. Your attitude! Your decisions! Your actions!

I hope the next few short chapters help create an atmosphere to help you have the right attitude, to make the right decisions, and to be able to turn these decisions into positive action.

COMMON SENSE MATTERS

Index of Thoughts on Life

Resilience... *Refuse to give in—or give up* 9
No Self-Limitations... *If you can dream it, you can do it* 13
Resolve... *The exhilaration of sticking to your guns and winning*............17
Passion... *The fire within*..21
Believe... *In the Supreme and yourself*..27
Self-Image... *The key to personality and behavior*...................................31
Five Steps to Self-Confidence... *Don't be positive you can't do it*......35
Excellence... *Is in the details*...39
Acceptance and Tolerance... *Of others and their beliefs* 43
Flex an Attitude Muscle... *Your attitude determines your altitude*.........47
Effort... *It does not matter how fast you travel, you will never see the sunrise if you are travelling west*...51
How You Think is Everything... *Make it positive* 55
Change Your Perspective... *It all depends on how you look at it*...........61
Train Your Brain... *Open up your mind and think*................................65
Financial and Emotional Wealth... *Takes basic "Un-Common Sense" to achieve results* 69
Do It Now... *Later is always too late* 73
Never Give Up... *Ability will only get you so far* 79
The Ethics of Excellence... *Never compromise your Personal Value System*..83
On Coaching... *Always HAVE a coach and BE a coach to others* 87
Choose Wisely... *Your life is a result of the choices you make* 93
Focus Your Time... *On the important, not the urgent* 97

Focus... *How do you know you've arrived if you didn't know where you were going in the first place*..*101*
Celebrate Victories... *Embrace the rewards* *105*

"Our greatest weakness lies in giving up. The most certain way to succeed is always to try just one more time."

Thomas A. Edison
American inventor & businessman

COMMON SENSE MATTERS

On Life

Resilience... *Refuse to give in—or give up*

Sooner or later in life, everyone experiences failure, disappointment, and setbacks or loses the desire to "keep on keeping on." One of the critical skills for ongoing success in life is the ability to bounce back from adversity.

Over the years I have had my share of failures—everyone has. I have learned that failing at a task doesn't make you a failure—the same way succeeding at a task doesn't make you a success. Many people have hit bottom, only to climb out of a hole and achieve greatness. And many people have done great things only to end up broke and alone, without any feeling of accomplishment.

The only true failure is failing to learn from your mistakes.

Success and failure are neutral concepts. What makes either of them positive or negative in life is not the event, circumstance, or situation, but rather what is done with them along the path of life. No one I have ever met has had a life filled only with success or failure. Resilience is the ability to keep coming back, again and again. No matter how many times life throws you a curve or brings you to your knees, you try again—you try something new, something different, or something old—in a new way.

In the 1920s there was a man named Mr. Eloff, who lived in South Africa. He believed there was gold in a certain area just west of Johannesburg. He sank every penny he had into mining for this gold. Over the years, all he ever found were small traces of the precious metal, so he decided to sell the mineral rights to the property—even though his geological training told him there was gold there. The man he was selling the rights to offered him the opportunity to retain a share of the company. Mr. Eloff had become so fed up with his lack of success he told his buyer he simply wanted out. He sold the mineral rights for a song, as the buyer was not a rich man either. Within six months of purchasing the rights, the new owner, Mr. Oppenheimer, hit the mother lode. To this day, the gold mine is one of the richest in the world. Mr. Oppenheimer went on to buy diamond mines and became one of the richest men in the world. Mr. Eloff died a poor man and his only claim to fame is the street in Johannesburg that bears his name. If only Mr. Eloff had not given up!

Follow your dream. Refuse to give in—or give up.

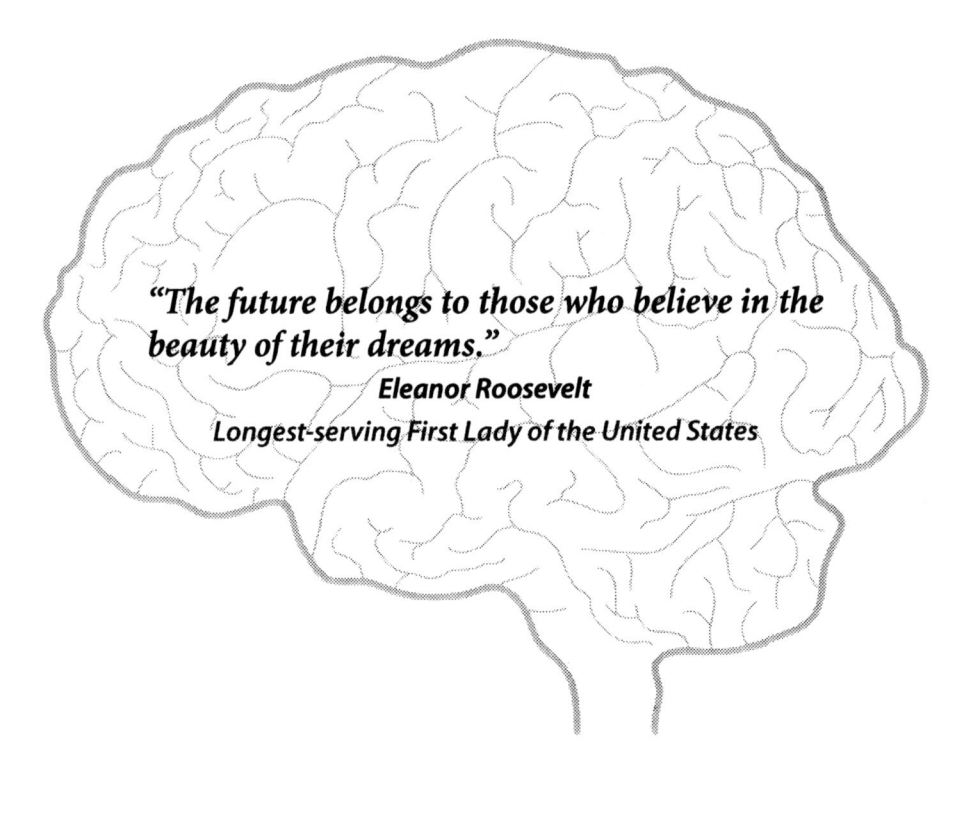

> "The future belongs to those who believe in the beauty of their dreams."
> *Eleanor Roosevelt*
> *Longest-serving First Lady of the United States*

COMMON SENSE MATTERS

On Life

No Self-Limitations… *If you can dream it, you can do it*

It has been said, by many people smarter than me, that "the only limitations we encounter in life are those we place on ourselves." This being true, why do so many people fail to reach their full potential? Why do so many people feel stuck, out of control, without hope in their lives?

Why do so many people give up, settle for less, and resign themselves to being an "also ran" when it comes to their quality of life? These people spend their lives blaming others, pointing their fingers toward something or someone or some circumstance that can be held responsible for their lack of success.

I have been at the bottom of the barrel in my life, many times. I have also reached the mountain tops and soared with eagles, many times. We are not inanimate objects. Why should we allow ourselves to be stuck in any business, relationship, job, way of life, or career that we are not enjoying, or is not fulfilling our needs and wants? Is it fear, comfort, procrastination, or even emotional manipulation by others?

Break out and be free!! Know what you want out of life and go get it. It takes courage, but the rewards are immeasurable. Each of us came into this world headed for greatness in some way, and yet, on the path of life, so many get conditioned for failure due to lack of faith in their own abilities.

Both self-limiting people and those with no self-limitations have dreams. The difference is that those with no self-limitations take those dreams and put them into ACTION.

There is a great person within each one of us. Accept that fact. All we need to do is recognize that person in ourselves.

> *A woman worked for me nearly forty years ago, whose eight-year-old daughter loved to play tennis. The kid was good. She wanted to be the best tennis player in the world. Her Mom told her that was probably not possible. The eight year old took a photograph of tennis legend Billie Jean King holding the Wimbledon Trophy above her head, cut out Billie Jean's face, and put a picture of her face in its place. Twelve years later this young lady not only played Wimbledon—she made it to the finals. WOW! Even at eight years old, the girl did not let her Mom's doubt influence her faith in herself.*

Are you living up to your full potential, or are you allowing fear to hold you back from the success you are imagining?

Have courage. Be strong. Believe in yourself. Have faith. You see you have no limitations, <u>because what the mind can conceive—it can achieve.</u>

Go for it…dream it…do it!

"I firmly believe that any man's finest hour, the greatest fulfillment of all he holds dear, is that moment when he has worked his heart out in a good cause and lies exhausted on the field of battle—victorious."

Vince Lombardi
American football player, coach & executive

COMMON SENSE MATTERS

On Life

Resolve... *The exhilaration of sticking to your guns and winning*

What is resolve? Is it persistence, commitment, dogged determination, or just plain old self-motivation? I don't have an answer to that. I do know, however, that it costs more to fail than to keep on keeping on. There is a point in every relationship, career, project, or goal where our resolve gets tested.

Winners realize that they have to break through this barrier before they can enjoy the real fruits of their labor. Quitters, on the other hand, give up at the first or second sign of resistance or adversity.

Thinking about quitting? A job? Career? Relationship? Project? Anything? Join the club. Sooner or later, everyone thinks about quitting something. There is, however, a vast difference between quitting and wanting to quit. Those with resolve think about it, then reassess why they set out on this path in the first place. They remotivate themselves, refocus on the end result, and get on with what they started out doing in the first place. Those who don't have resolve, simply quit. Sometimes it is laziness, sometimes it is cowardice, sometimes it is just the lack of drive that prevents them from starting again. *Don't give up.* Be resolute; focus on what can be.

On Life

My relationship with my dad was a very unfortunate one. We did not see eye to eye, at all. It was serious stuff. I was at an airport when my wife called me to tell me he had passed on. We hadn't spoken for some time…yet I cried. And I realized later that the reason for my tears was not because of my loss, but rather because of what could have been, and I questioned whether I had shown enough resolve over the past forty years to put things right between us. Did I give up too soon for any of the reasons I have mentioned above?

I have given up. I know the consequences of failure. I know how it feels to abandon a dream.

I wanted to be a doctor when I was a young man. That was my dream. I had many obstacles in my way at the time. My parents' lack of finances. The necessity of getting a job to help support my grandparents. Only average grades at school (because I didn't resolve to work hard enough). These circumstances contributed to my throwing in the towel. But now I know, I COULD HAVE FOUND A WAY to become a doctor. I gave up too soon. I settled for second, or third, best—because it was easier. I could have worked harder, secured a second (or third) job and simply put in more effort. But this taught me a lesson. Now, I know the thrill of overcoming difficulties and the benefits of resolve. From having had to elope to spend my life with the woman I love (we have now been married for over fifty four years) to reaching great heights in two careers—after only having two meals a day, walking miles every day to get to work, and my wife having to flirt with the butcher to get an extra steak thrown in the shopping bag—we are now (and have been for years) in the best place we could ever imagine!

We had resolve. We made up our minds. We did not take our eyes off the ball. And we know you don't spell "success" c-a-s-h (even though it helps).

There are many to ways to spell success...one is r-e-s-o-l-v-e.

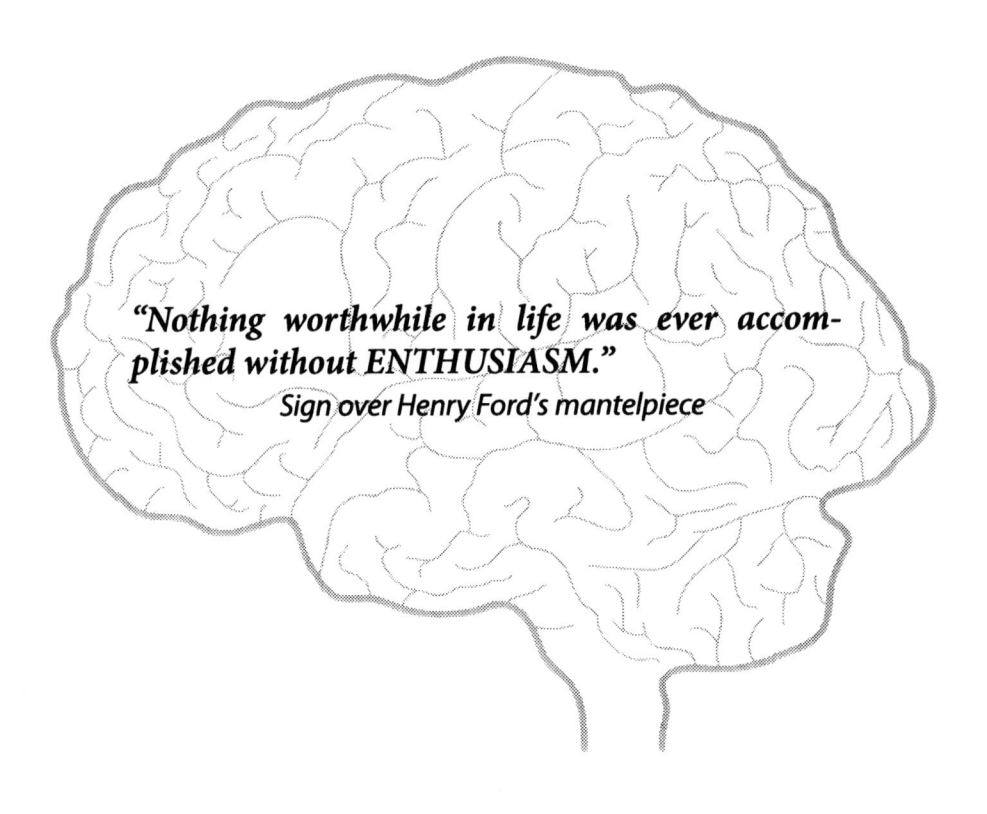

> *"Nothing worthwhile in life was ever accomplished without ENTHUSIASM."*
> Sign over Henry Ford's mantelpiece

COMMON SENSE MATTERS

On Life

Passion...*the fire within*

Whether we call it *enthusiasm* or *passion* is relatively unimportant. What is important, however, is that we have that burning desire to succeed permeating throughout our entire being. There are many examples of people who realized success because of a deeply rooted passion, but I would like to focus on one.

Steve Jobs founded Apple in 1976. He revolutionized our lives by making the computer personal. Let's take a brief look at the man and the passion that drove him to change the world as we know it today. Macintosh; music with the iPod and iTunes; mobile with the iPhone; tablets with the iPad; and digital animation with Pixar.

> Jobs was ousted from the company he founded, built, and loved. He was invited, asked, begged to come back when it was not performing well. He returned, rebuilt it with a vengeance, and relaunched it with the mantra, "THINK DIFFERENT." He was heard to say, in his commencement address at Stanford University in 2005, "Remembering that you are going to die is the best way I know to avoid the trap of thinking you have something to lose. You are already naked. There is no reason not to follow your heart...Stay hungry. Stay foolish."

Jobs always believed he would die young. He passed away at age fifty-six, in October of 2011. He knew that he needed a burning passion to achieve what he had in his heart before he left us. He had five major tenants that he lived by, and we can certainly use them in our lives:

1. **Take action NOW** because the clock is ticking. Our time here is finite. When we lose a minute, an hour, a year being unproductive, it is gone forever. We can never get it back.

2. **Make a memorable first impression.** When Apple sprang the Apple II at the West Coast Computer Faire in 1977, Jobs secured a booth at the front of the exhibit hall and made the display dramatic. He draped the exhibit in black velvet, imprinted with his new logo. He put only three Apple IIs on display (the only three he had finished), and he piled empty product boxes on the rest of the stand, to give the impression many more were on hand. What a first impression!

3. **Link with "A-Plus" Teammates.** Associate with like-minded people who also have a passion for whatever they do. You will feed off each other. You will motivate each other. Find people that you would like to emulate and spend time with them. One of the things I regret most in my life is that I have never had a mentor. It is for this reason I have always sought out successful, passionate people.

4. **Focus on a few things and do them well.** Do not be a "Jack-of-all-trades and a master of none." Focus. The same way a sheet of glass, held over paper in full sunlight, will not burn the paper—yet a magnifying glass held over the same piece of paper with

half the sunlight will make the paper burst into flame—so will your focus on fewer facets in your life bring you greater results.

Go with your gut. Steve Jobs always shunned market research. He said market research told you what people wanted. He contended he wanted to give people what they will want in the **future**.

Passion is not an act. It is a way of believing. It is woven into your cellular structure just as much as your DNA. Passion—real passion—for who you are and who you are becoming; where you are and where you are going; what you believe; what you stand for and would die for—shouts to the world: "I am here to stay. I am here to make a difference. I will leave my mark in this world. It may take my entire life, but I will not give up until my purpose and destiny are realized."

Passion is the great equalizer. It can, in part, make up for lack of experience and knowledge. I am not suggesting that you not develop your knowledge or experience—only that when your experience is a little lacking, your passion will be interpreted by others as a strong belief in yourself, your mission, and your purpose. Nothing great in life was ever achieved without enthusiasm and passion.

> *Billionaire Mark Cuban (owner of the Dallas Mavericks) says, "Sweat equity is the most valuable equity there is. Know your business and know your industry better than anyone else in the world. Love what you do with a passion—or don't do it."*

You can see it in peoples eyes, hear it in their voice, and sense it in their behavior. How are you doing? Are you in love with where you are, where you are going, who you are becoming, and what you are contributing? Or, are you living like more than 85 percent of the population with the attitude, "Same Stuff, Different Day"? If you have lost or are losing your passion for your life, your career, or a relationship, *do whatever is necessary to get it back*. Here are a few ideas to consider:

Focus on Life's Blessings. Don't dwell on life's trials and tribulations. Focus on your blessings and your goals. Try this one on for size: "I used to complain that I had no shoes, until I met a man who had no feet."

The power of positive thinking is a great philosophy. However, if you sit in a chair and think positively about being wealthy, it will never happen unless you get up out of that chair AND DO SOMETHING. So it is the *Power of Positive Doing* that will energize you and give you the enthusiasm and passion that will lead to your life's success. Be active. Do something that puts a spring in your step and a glint in your eye.

It sometimes takes courage to let go of old baggage. As Nike says, "Just do it." Life is constantly changing—particularly for those of us who have a passion for success and achievement. But in the ebb and flow of life, what may have been useful in yesteryear may no longer be useful today. You do not need to carry this old baggage with you for the rest of your life. The lighter your load, the easier it will be to passionately travel toward today's goals. Be strong. Have courage. Get rid of your old baggage.

Accept the reality of a situation with an open mind. Then, with an open mind, you will be able to make decisions to change or capitalize on these situations.

> *How about Oscar Pistorius, the South African who competed in the 2012 Olympics? He is a double amputee (both his legs were amputated below the knees at eleven months old) who refused*

to accept the fact that he was "handicapped." He maintained he was merely "different." Even after being disqualified from the 2008 Olympics, he would not be deterred. He believed in himself and talked himself into fighting to take his place in the 2012 Olympics. His belief took him not only into the Men's 400-meter Race, but also on to South Africa's Men's 4 × 400-meter relay team. Oscar Pistorius has a passion for running. Unfortunately, and infamously, he lost his focus on success and misdirected his passion, to his detriment.*

Do everything you do with passion. Don't be halfhearted in any of your activities or endeavors. Give 101 percent all the time. It will not only affect the outcome of *your* life—this drive is infectious—it will influence the behaviors of those with whom you come into contact. Surround yourself with people who are passionate about their lot in life.

Henry Ford had a similar philosophy. Ford always said if he gave people what they wanted it would have been a faster horse and the automobile would never have made it to market. Go with your gut!

Keep your passion alive!

*Oscar Pistorius also serves as a cautionary tale on the power of passion. On St. Valentine's Day in 2013, Pistorius shot and killed his girlfriend, Reeva Steenkamp, at his home in South Africa. While circumstances do not diminish his accomplishments, they do negate the respect we have for the man.

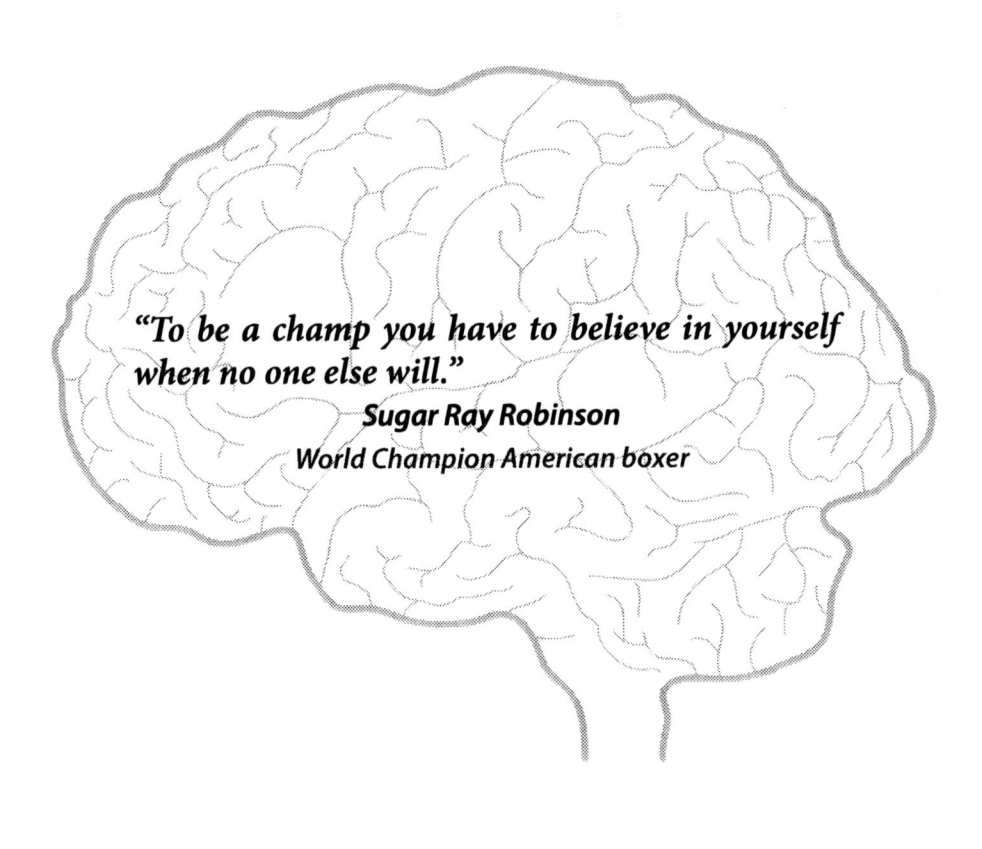

> "To be a champ you have to believe in yourself when no one else will."
> *Sugar Ray Robinson*
> World Champion American boxer

COMMON SENSE MATTERS

On Life

Believe...In the Supreme and yourself

In 1960, Dr. Maxwell Maltz, a world-famous plastic surgeon, wrote a book entitled *Psycho Cybernetics*. It stemmed from a study he conducted based on his observation that the plastic surgery patients who did not have a positive self-image to begin with were never happy with the external improvements he was making for them. The truth is that if a person has a negative self-image, even the best plastic surgeon in the world would not be able to help them. In my opinion, this is one of the best books ever written on the psychological aspects of self-improvement. To this day, I keep this book next to my bed and from time to time pick it up and reread a paragraph, a page, or chapter when I am in need of some help to inspire me or to "right the ship." Without any doubt, for me, the best chapter in the book is entitled, **"Look at Yourself with Kind Eyes."** Just think of this for a minute, and it won't need any explanation. We all tend to beat up on ourselves when things are not going well. We look at all our shortcomings and very seldom look at what we do that is right. Sometimes, we find that our loved ones—or people we respect—may not realize we need a little lift, and this is when we have to *give it to ourselves.*

We have to learn to like ourselves and respect ourselves, because if we don't, we cannot expect others to like or respect us. There must be more books written on this subject than just about anything else, but

I do not know of any others that talk about looking at yourself with kind eyes.
Be kind to yourself; forgive yourself when need be. *Like who you are.* Look at your virtues and forgive your shortcomings.

And talking about liking yourself, I must share this story with you. It is the single most important story that has influenced my life:

> *Some years ago, a sales trainer, Larry Nelson, visited the Hopi Indian Reservation. He spent six months with them. When saying his goodbyes, the Matriarch of the Tribe, a wonderfully wizened old woman, approached him. She wanted to express how she felt about him. She was searching for the right words, then slowly, hesitatingly, said, "<u>I like me best...when I am with you.</u>" Oh, My Goodness! If only we could go through life like that. If we could make people feel that way about us. If only we could feel that way about ourselves, the world would be our oyster.*

I believe that religion is a deeply personal and private affair, not suited for discussion in an open forum, but I feel it is incumbent on me to share a thought with you. I always feel there is an "Invisible Hand" guiding us. That everything that happens in our lives is preordained. That the Lord is always there looking after us. I believe that our souls are from the same essence as the Lord. He is the Ocean and we are the drops. When our belief in the Lord is strong, so is our belief in ourselves. Then being strong and successful, however we may define success, is within our grasp...because we believe.

> *For those who believe, no proof is necessary.*
> *For those who don't believe, no proof is possible.*
> Stuart Chase, Writer and Economist

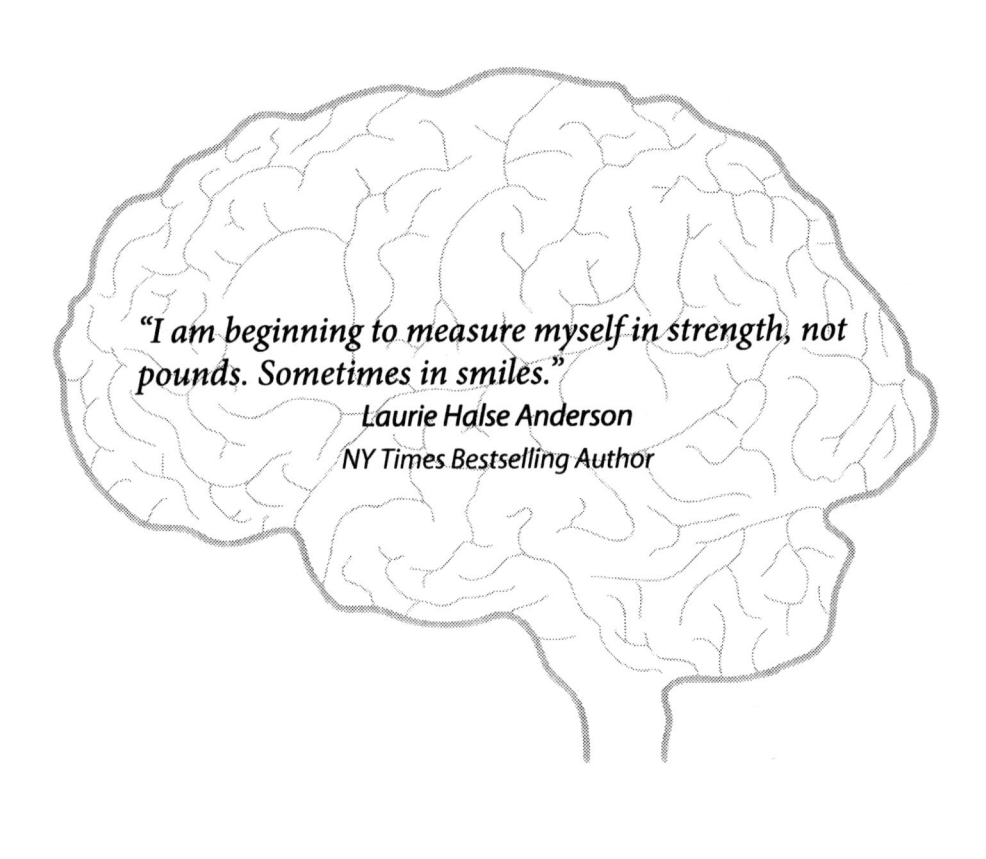

> "I am beginning to measure myself in strength, not pounds. Sometimes in smiles."
> Laurie Halse Anderson
> NY Times Bestselling Author

COMMON SENSE MATTERS

On Life

Self-Image... The key to personality and behavior

Change your self-image and you will change your personality and your behavior patterns.
Self-image sets the boundaries of individual accomplishment. It defines what you can and cannot do. Expand your self-image, and you expand what you can achieve. Expand your self-image and you expand the *area of the possible*. The development of a realistic and adequate self-image can turn failure into success.

Self-image psychology has not only been proven on its own merits, it also explains many phenomena that have long been known, but not properly understood. There is irrefutable clinical evidence in both psychosomatic medicine and industrial psychology that there are *success type* personalities and *failure type* personalities. There are *happiness prone* personalities and *unhappiness prone* personalities. There are *health prone* personalities and *disease prone* personalities. Self-image psychology throws a new light on the power of positive thinking, and more importantly, explains why it works with some individuals and not with others. Positive thinking will indeed work when it is consistent with your self-image. By the same token, it cannot work if it is inconsistent with your self-image—until it has been changed.

On Life

The changing of your self-image can be a wonderfully successful journey as you start to enjoy new experiences and successes in life. A great starting point for you would be to read Dr. Maxwell Maltz's book, *Psycho-Cybernetics*, as mentioned in the previous chapter.

To share some thoughts with you on what self-image can do for a person, I could not think of a better example than the first time I met with Mohammed Ali. I had the good fortune to have dinner with him in New York in 1979, at the home of boxing enthusiast Jim Jacobs and his wife, Lorraine.

The persona that we know as Mohammed Ali would typically not be considered a deep thinker. Yet he was. We spent most of the night talking about "stuff" that had nothing to do with boxing. Ali said that after he won the gold medal at the 1960 Olympic Games (as a light heavyweight, still known as Cassius Clay) he knew he could be the greatest boxer that ever lived. He knew it in depths of his soul. He could feel it. He could taste it. Now all he had to do was market himself to the world.

He also knew, he said, that he had a challenge. And that challenge was that there were two sides to him. One had to be the smooth-talking, braggadocios warrior; the other was a nice guy with deep thoughts that he wanted to live by. He had two self-images. The one was being "The Greatest"—the boxer that could "float like a butterfly and sting like a bee." The other was the man that quipped, "Silence is golden—when you can't think of a good answer." He was the nineteen-year-old who came back from the Olympics with the gold and walked into a luncheonette in Louisville, Kentucky, where blacks were not permitted to eat. He sat down, with his gold medal around his neck, and ordered a meal. He was told, "We don't serve ni**ers here." He responded, "Don't worry, I don't eat them." He left the luncheonette disgusted. Ali walked down to the Ohio River, took his gold medal from around his neck, and threw it into the water.

This icon is a man who possesses two self-images. He fits them both and has always had the ability to wear them with dignity. As he left Jim's apartment that night, he shook my hand and said, "If people would love each other the way they love me—what a great world this would be." You just gotta love it!

"People are crying up the rich and variegated plumage of the peacock, and he is himself blushing at the sight of his ugly feet."

Saadi Shiraz
Major Persian Sufi poet of the medieval period

Believe yourself beautiful, strong, and successful!

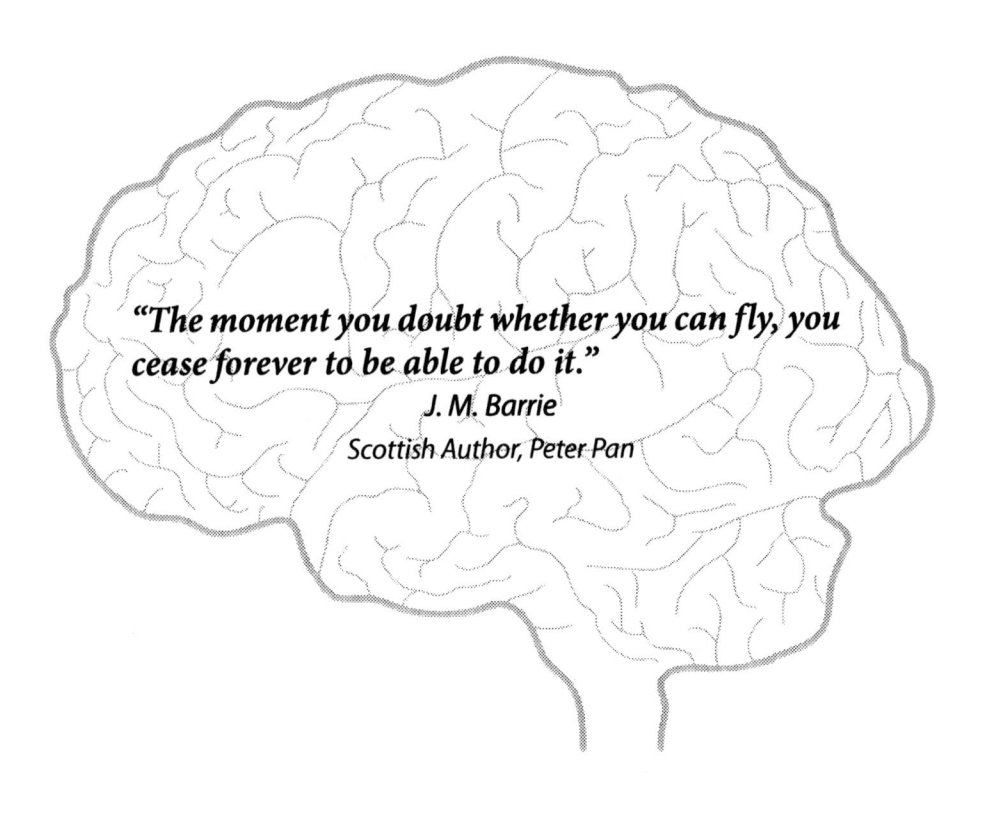

"The moment you doubt whether you can fly, you cease forever to be able to do it."
J. M. Barrie
Scottish Author, Peter Pan

COMMON SENSE MATTERS

On Life

Five Steps to Self-Confidence...Don't be positive you can't do it

Self-confidence comes from success—no matter how small. Success comes from continuous improvement. Improvement comes from dedication. Dedication comes from a burning desire to achieve a goal.

Self-confidence is quiet. It comes from within. It is not loudness; it is not bravado, and it is not arrogance. Sometimes, these acts are viewed by others as self-confidence. But more often than not, the opposite is true. It is arrogance hiding the lack of confidence. Just as strength of character comes from within, so does self-confidence. A deep-rooted belief in one's ability to perform in the most difficult of situations results in self-confidence.

I challenge you to read these five declarations every day for thirty days and program your sub-conscious to self-belief:

1. ***I know that I have the ability to achieve my purpose or goal in life.***
   I demand of myself persistent, continuous action toward attainment and promise myself to render such action.

2. ***I realize my dominating thoughts will eventually lead to action and gradually, into physical reality.*** Therefore, I will concentrate for thirty minutes daily on my goals and what I will feel like when I achieve them.

3. ***I will embrace, through autosuggestion, any goal I persistently retain in my mind.*** I will eventually seek fruition through some practical means.

4. ***I have clearly written down a description of my chief goals in life.***
   I visualize myself as having achieved them. I have the knowledge that my sub-conscious is programmed to recognize these successes and, consequently, give me self-confidence.

5. ***I will engage in no transaction which does not benefit all whom it affects.***
   - I fully realize that no wealth or position can long endure unless built upon truth and justice.
   - I will succeed by attracting to myself the forces I wish to use and the cooperation of other people.
   - I will induce others to serve me because of my willingness to serve others.
   - I will eliminate hatred, envy, jealousy, selfishness, and cynicism by developing love for all humanity, because I know that a negative attitude toward others can never bring me success. I will cause others to believe in me because I will believe in them and in myself.

6. **I will sign my name to this formula, commit it to memory, and _repeat it aloud once a day_**, with full faith that it will gradually influence my thoughts and actions so that I will become a self-reliant and successful person.

In 1979, over dinner in New York with boxing icons Jimmy Jacobs and Mohammed Ali, I asked "The Champ" a question. "Why," I wondered, "when you were building up to your first world title fight, did you predict the round in which you would stop your opponent?" (And he delivered...he rarely ever missed!!) He said it was because he had total belief in his ability to do what he set his mind to, and that it programmed his sub-conscious to accept nothing less. This gave him the self-confidence and belief in himself that he simply would not fail.

> *Everyone is endowed with a talent.*
> *Find that talent in yourself.*
> *Recognize it. Respect it. Build on it.*

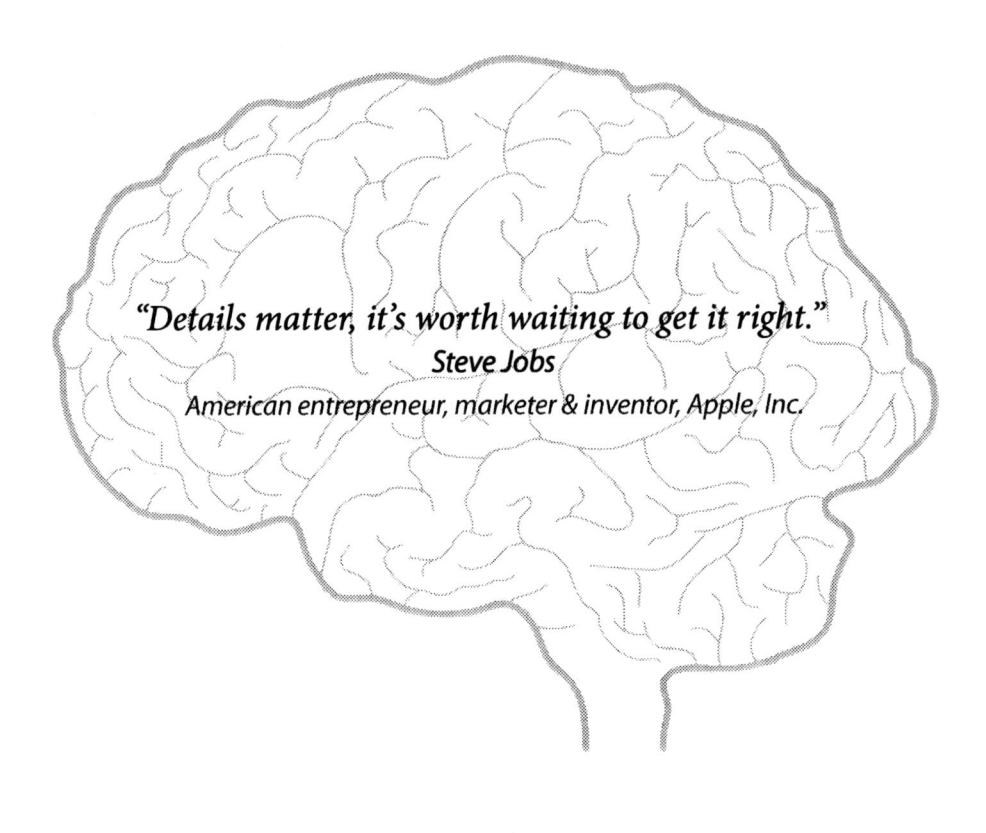

"Details matter, it's worth waiting to get it right."
Steve Jobs
American entrepreneur, marketer & inventor, Apple, Inc.

COMMON SENSE MATTERS

On Life

Excellence...Is in the details

Dr. Richard Carlson, a renowned psychologist, wrote a book entitled, *Don't Sweat the Small Stuff*. He made an awful lot of money with this book because most people are too darn lazy to take time to *sweat the small stuff*. Excellence is in the details, period. Have you ever observed an airline pilot preparing for takeoff? He has been flying for possibly twenty years and has taken off probably eight to ten thousand times—and he still goes through the check list **every time he takes off**. Would you rather have a surgeon operating on you that does not sweat the small stuff or one that knows excellence is in the details?

When we talk morals and ethics, this principle in life becomes even more magnified. How can we be trusted with big things in life if we're not trustworthy with the small ones?

In the ethics of excellence, everything you do counts. The most minor violations weaken your reputation for rightness. As Tom Peters says in *Thriving on Chaos*, "Integrity may be about little things as much or more than big ones."

> In 1979, my promotions company promoted a world boxing title fight. We anticipated 100,000 people to attend. It was staged in a rugby stadium that only had 65,000 seats. So we had to

place over 35,000 seats on the field. Prior to this, our largest promotion only had 40,000 attendees, and this was a major challenge. Our most successful promotions were those that accommodated about 20,000 people—this way we could attend to the minutest detail—so how could we cope with a 100,000 seat promotion? Well, what we did to achieve excellence and have every detail perfect was to build five 20,000 seat stadiums in the one venue. Everything from toilets to hot dog stands; from entrances to amenity kiosks; from hidden security (we had six heads of state in attendance) to entertainment bands. The end result was that the promotion, in its time, was the largest-grossing boxing tournament ever staged. Our promotion company received accolades in the world sports press for its excellence. Yes, excellence was in the details.

Learn to analyze the details. Get all the facts, all the input. Learn from your mistakes. Oliver Perry, a US Naval hero in the war of 1812, took over America's mission at Lake Erie when he was twenty-seven. He overcame the Royal Navy, considered the greatest fleet in the world. He famously summarized his strategy: "Solid planning and attention to detail will always boost the underdog. We have met the enemy and now they are ours."

Aristotle once said, "We are what we repeatedly do. Excellence, therefore, is not an act, but a habit." So does doing something over and over make you perfect? Not necessarily. The key is learning to practice correctly. **We have heard it said many times: "Practice does not make perfect. Only perfect practice makes perfect."** Repeatedly focus on attending to the details of whatever you do if you want to achieve excellence.

COMMON SENSE MATTERS

So sweat the small stuff. Take care of the little things and the big things will take care of themselves... because excellence is in the details.

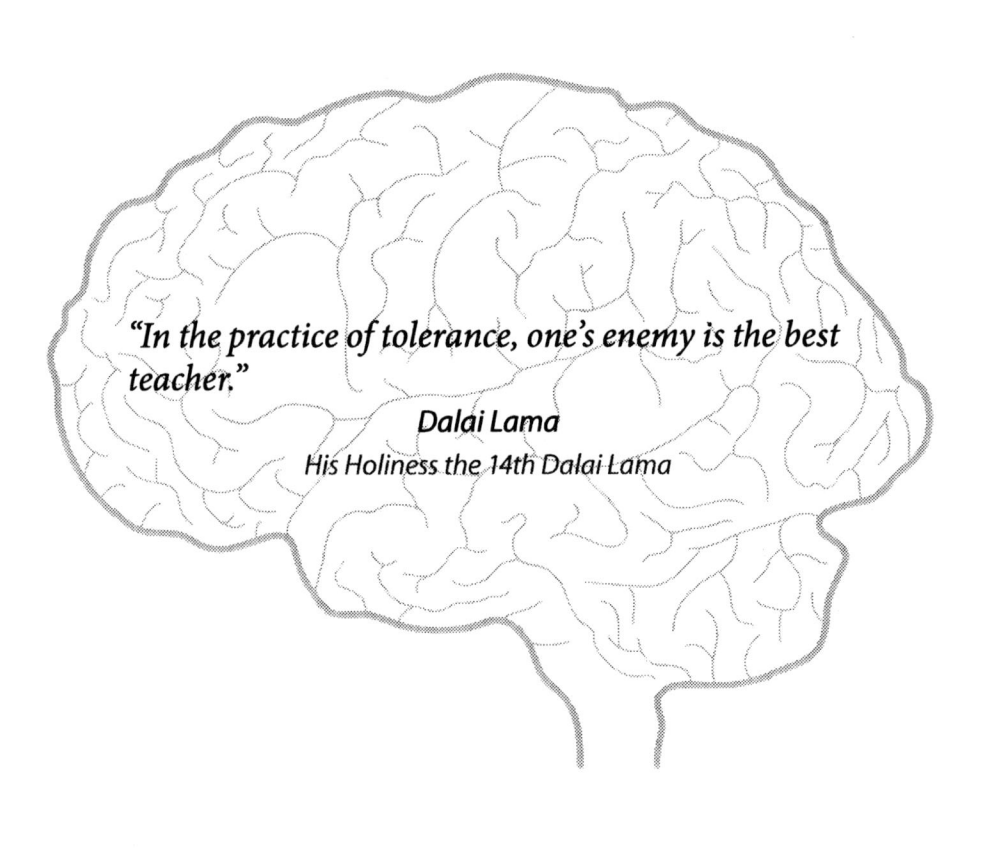

"In the practice of tolerance, one's enemy is the best teacher."

Dalai Lama
His Holiness the 14th Dalai Lama

COMMON SENSE MATTERS

On Life

Acceptance and Tolerance... Of others and their beliefs

As I have said previously, I was born in South Africa and moved to the United States in 1981. My wife and I tried to make this move in 1959, but, unfortunately, the American Immigration Policy was on a quota system and we had to wait twenty-one years before we restructured our lives so that we were able to come here legally. The reason I am telling you this is because our reason for wanting to immigrate was the total intolerance of the South African government and the consequential implementation of the policy of apartheid. I do not want to talk politics, but I do want to talk about *tolerance*. They go hand in glove, and I feel the best way for me to express my feelings is to share with you exerpts of what Ben Stein said on CBS one Sunday Morning—as it relates to tolerance. In my mind, Mr. Stein is one of the best commentators in the media today, and I believe he expresses the *ambience* of tolerance in the following words:

> My Confession:
> I am a Jew, and every single one of my ancestors was Jewish. And it does not bother me even a little bit when people call those beautiful lit up, bejeweled trees, Christmas trees. I don't feel threatened. I don't feel discriminated against. That's what they are, Christmas trees.

It does not bother me a bit when people say, "Merry Christmas", to me. I don't think they are slighting me, or getting ready to put me in a ghetto. In fact I kind of like it. It shows we are all brothers and sister celebrating a happy time of the year. It doesn't bother me at all that there is a manger scene at a key intersection near my beach house in Malibu. If people want a crèche it's just as fine with me, as is the Menorah a few hundred yards away.

I don't like getting pushed around for being a Jew, and I don't think Christians like being pushed around for being Christians. I think people who believe in God are sick and tired of being pushed around, period. I have no idea where the concept came from, that America is an explicitly atheist country. I can't find it in the Constitution and I don't like it being shoved down my throat.

Or maybe I can put another way: where did the idea come from that we should worship celebrities and we aren't allowed to worship God as we understand Him? I guess that's a sign that I am getting old, too. But there are a lot of us wondering where celebrities came from, and where the America we knew went to.

Dr. Benjamin Spock said we shouldn't spank our children when they misbehave, because their little personalities might get warped and we might damage their self-esteem (Dr. Spock committed suicide). We said an expert should know what he is talking about. And we said OK.
Now we are asking ourselves why our children have no conscience, why they don't know right from wrong, and why it doesn't bother them to kill strangers, their classmates, and themselves.

Probably if we think about it long and hard enough we will figure out it has a lot to do with, WE REAP WHAT WE SOW.

I personally believe that tolerance and acceptance go hand in glove. To tolerate or accept something—a person or situation, for example—does not mean you have to like it. Having the ability to accept and tolerate can save us much angst. If we rail and kick against it and grow bitter, we still won't change the inevitable. I learned this at an early age when I realized that whatever I did or said, my parents would not accept the woman I had chosen to be my wife. I had to accept that the inevitable choice I was about to make would cost me my relationship with my parents. I was a fool and railed and rebelled against it. I turned nights of hell into insomnia. I brought upon myself everything I didn't want. Finally, I had to accept what I knew from the outset I couldn't possibly alter. And once I had accepted this—and was prepared to accept the consequences—my life turned around, as this weight was lifted off my shoulders.

In life, we get the behavior from people and the results from situations that we are prepared to tolerate.

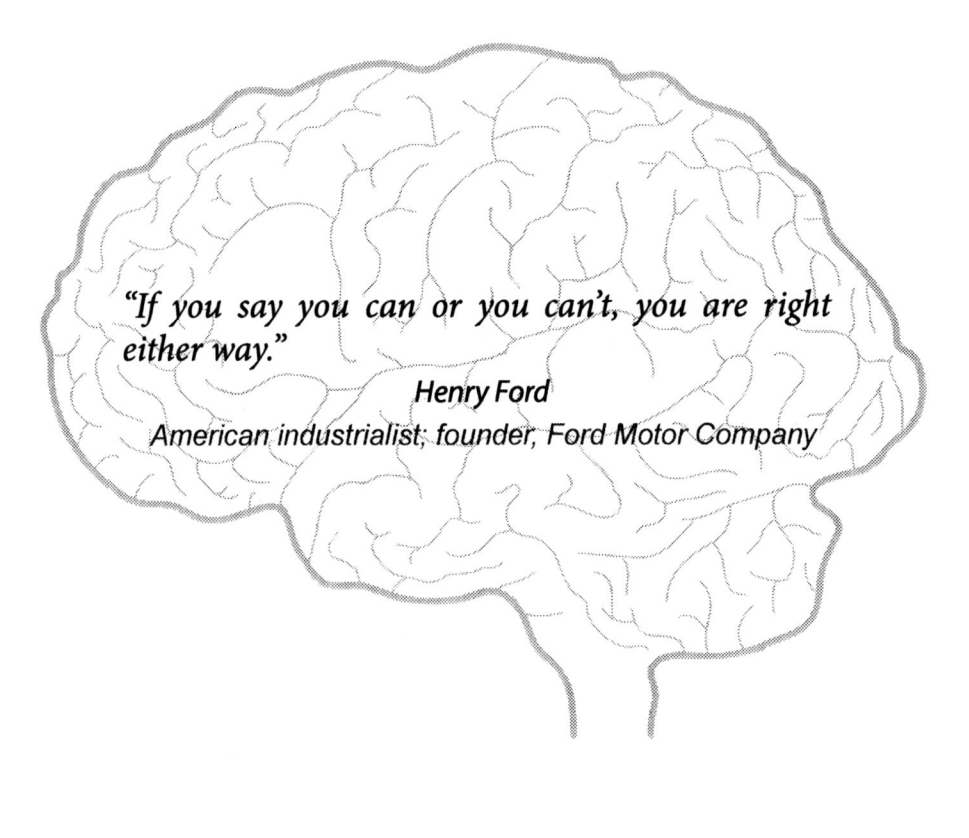

"If you say you can or you can't, you are right either way."

Henry Ford
American industrialist; founder, Ford Motor Company

COMMON SENSE MATTERS

On Life

Flex an Attitude Muscle... *Your attitude determines your altitude*

Some people are naturally upbeat. Others develop that can-do attitude. Let's take a look at how to develop *emotional brawn*.

Self-confidence and optimism are very closely linked. In life, we can boost our mental might so big challenges are not daunting. We have the ability to face any adversity and make things better.

Muscle is built by repetition. And as a training exercise for our mind, we need repetition as well. There are three questions you should ask yourself (and answer) every night. But remember to do it *out loud*. You want the questions and answers to penetrate into your subconscious. They are:

- What did I do well today?
- What can I improve tomorrow?
- What is one specific thing that I can do to make that happen?

This may sound a bit soft to you at first—but believe me, it will condition your subconscious and shift your mentality. About forty-five years ago, I read *Think and Grow Rich* by Napoleon Hill. In it he explained how one should write down their goals and set a timeframe in which they should be achieved, then read them aloud first thing every morning and last thing every night. I chuckled to myself, thinking, "This will never work." But I did it. Every evening I repeated my goals so I could hear what I was saying. Then on the way to work, I said them really loud and repeated them many times. People laughed at me when they saw me talking to myself at traffic lights. But you know what? IT WORKED. I hit all three of the goals I set for myself, with months to spare.

You do the same with the three questions I have given you above. But remember to include the answers.

Remember not to dwell on your flaws. Don't focus on your screw-ups. Recognize what you did well and relentlessly pursue improvement.

When you mess up, have the discipline not to make excuses. It is OK for you to come up short sometimes.

Excuses are the antithesis of growth. In the long run, you will feel better if you suck it up. Allow yourself to feel pain and use it as a motivator to do better.

***If you make a mistake, own it,
learn from it, and never make the same one again!***

"Satisfaction lies in the effort, not in the attainment. Full effort is full victory."
Mahatma Gandhi
Considered the father of the Indian independence movement

COMMON SENSE MATTERS

On Life

Effort... *It does not matter how fast you travel; you will not see the sun rise if you are travelling west*

We have heard it for years: Work smarter. Work more efficiently. Work more creatively.

These philosophies are all valid and deserve respect and serious consideration, but whatever happened to old-fashioned hard work? I am not advocating a seventy-hour work week—sacrificing family, friends, or personal interests—or joining Workaholics Anonymous!

You can work smarter and more effectively, but I don't believe there is any substitute for effort and doing whatever it takes to achieve your goals, mission, and purpose in life. I believe in a balanced life. I believe there are other worthy elements in life besides work, career, or running your business, which deserve your effort.

- √ If you earn a living by doing physical labor, give it everything you've got—all the time. Put in the effort.
- √ If your position is one of leadership or management, your effort may be in thinking, planning, solving problems, but this too takes effort and much discipline.
- √ Put in the effort to pray and to meditate.

- ✓ Put in the effort and practice for recreational activities, or don't complain that you are not good enough or that no one wants to play with you.
- ✓ Put in the effort to be a good parent, child, husband, or wife. This takes more effort than anything else.

When I say, "Put in the effort," I mean in life in general, not only in what you do for a living. There are many areas of life that deserve your efforts, besides your career.

Put in the effort to:

- Give your life a sense of meaning. Have a *spiritual goal,* as well as a material goal, that is measurable.
- Give yourself a creative outlet for your talent. Take time to do something for yourself. Do things in life you love, not only things you *have to.*
- Build your self-esteem. Look at yourself with *kind eyes.*
- Keep from being bored. Always be doing something, whether it's a physical activity or a crossword puzzle.
- Broaden your contacts and the opportunity for friends. Embrace *social contact* as well as *social media.*

Contribute to your personal development. Educate yourself. Learn. Grow. If I could get a college degree at sixty-five, then what is stopping you?

In 1982, Mickey Mantle was meeting with my wife and me at dinner to finalize a promotion for my company. Having come from South Africa, where baseball was not played, we knew nothing of the sport. Mickey loved the idea that we did not *know he was an American icon. He thought the very simple questions we asked him were a hoot. At one stage, I asked him what, in his opinion, his greatest asset was in the game he loved so much. He said, <u>"I was persistent. I put in the effort and worked hard. In short, I never stopped swinging."</u> This comes from a man whose career was plagued by injuries. He went on to say (and I am paraphrasing here), "People must learn to deal with hardships head on, not make excuses, and let your teammates know they can depend on you. I love the game of baseball, but it is so much easier to love when my legs don't hurt."*

This effort will not only help you succeed, but also to live longer!

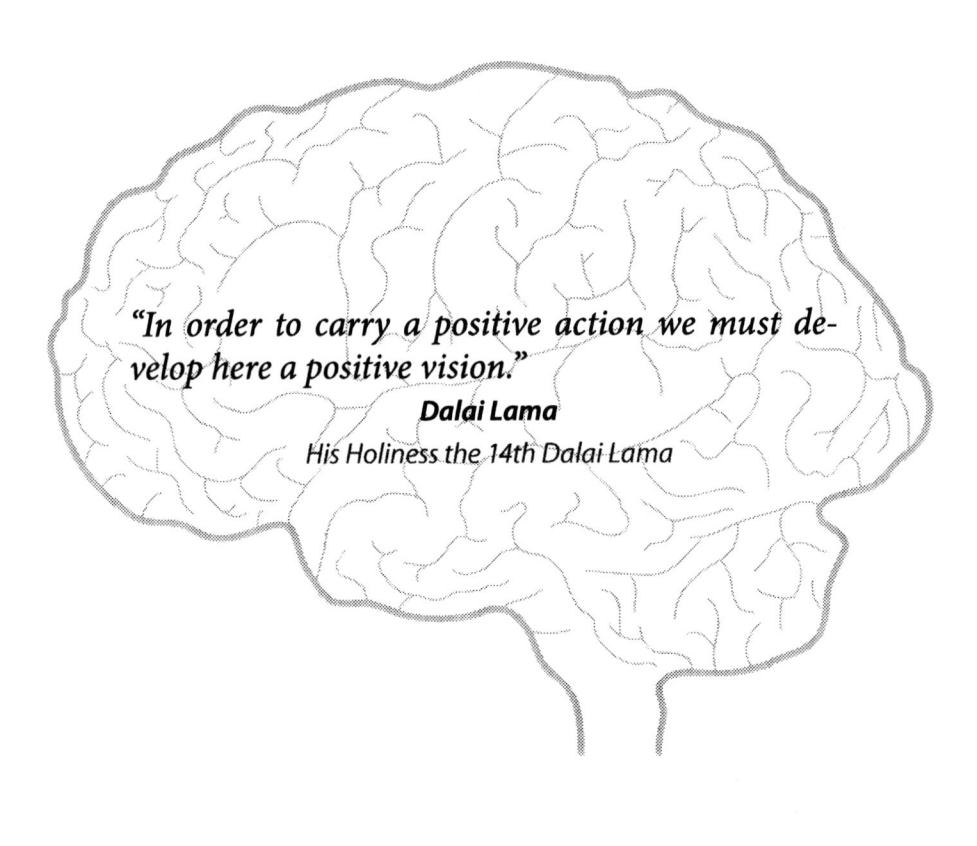

"In order to carry a positive action we must develop here a positive vision."
Dalai Lama
His Holiness the 14th Dalai Lama

COMMON SENSE MATTERS

On Life

How You Think is Everything... Make it positive

Always be positive. Think success, not failure. Beware of a negative environment.

Aim higher. "Winning changes nothing," says performance psychologist Jim Loehr. "I've heard those words repeated many times." The Human Performance Institute he cofounded helps executives and top athletes peak professionally. "There are promises that society makes about where we will find our happiness and fulfillment," Loehr says. Top status? Fame? Money? According to Loehr, these stereotypical motivators will only take us so far.

True champions look for something more—and they find the ultimate result is personal. "The highest order of concern for nearly everyone is how they treated others. That will be the most important scorecard in life."

Relish the journey. If you are an entrepreneur, you have to relish the rush you get from building—not the paycheck. Otherwise the work is too hard and the sacrifices too great. You don't want to believe that building a business and selling it for a million dollars is the Holy Grail. You want to enjoy the journey.

Eli Broad, CEO of numerous Fortune 500 companies and the author of *The Art of Being Unreasonable,* shared that **"All of my careers have required me to be quite unreasonable—to have an outsized ambition, discipline, energy, and the focus to have the confidence to ignore people who said I couldn't do it."**

Stay hungry. At seventy-nine, Broad is still going strong. His sentiments are that whether it is your job, your philanthropy, or your pursuit of knowledge—your job is never done.

> *When my son was three years old I gave him a copy of Rudyard Kipling's (1909) poem "IF." I had it transposed in calligraphy on aged parchment. I have since given it to my grandsons and to people who I believed could benefit from it. If you can "think" the essence of this poem, you will be an amazing person, my friend.*

Common Sense Matters

IF

If you can keep your head when all about you are
Losing theirs, and blaming it on you;
If you can trust yourself when all men doubt you,
But make allowance for their doubting too;
If you can wait, and not be tired by waiting,
Or being lied about, don't deal in lies;
Or being hated, don't give way to hating,
And yet, don't look too good or talk too wise.

If you can dream—and not make dreams your master,
If you can think—and not make thoughts your aim;
If you can meet with triumph and disaster,
And treat those two imposters just the same;
If you can bear to hear the Truth you have spoken
Twisted by knaves to make a trap for fools;
Or watch the things you gave your life to, broken,
And stoop and build them up with worn out tools;

If you can make one heap of all your winnings,
And risk it on one turn of pitch-and-toss,
And lose, and start again at your beginnings
And never breathe a word about your loss;
If you can force your heart and nerve and sinew
To serve your turn long after they have gone,
And hold on when there is nothing in you
Except the Will which says to them "Hold On!"

If you can talk with crowds and keep your virtue
Or walk with Kings—nor lose the common touch,

On Life

If neither foes nor loving friends can hurt you,
If all men count with you—but none too much;
If you can fill the unforgiving minute
With sixty seconds' worth of distance run,
Yours is the Earth and everything that's in it,
And—which is more—
You'll be a man my Son.

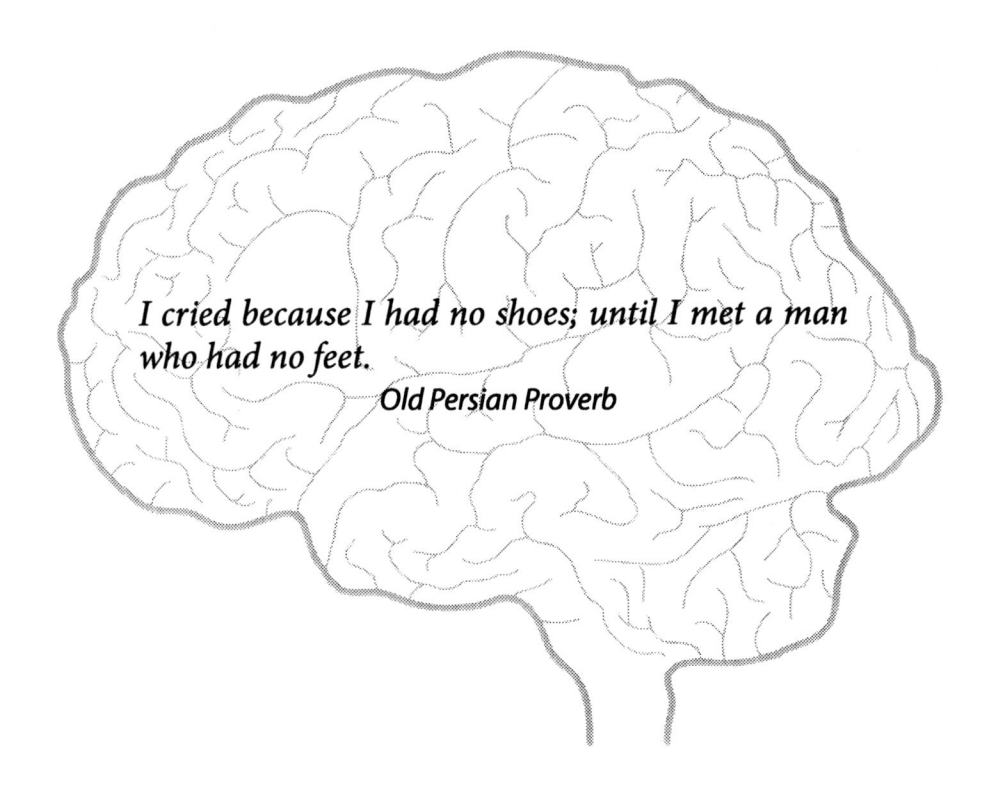

I cried because I had no shoes; until I met a man who had no feet.
　　　　　Old Persian Proverb

COMMON SENSE MATTERS

On Life

Change Your Perspective...*It all depends on how you look at it*

Sometimes telling a short story gets a message across more succinctly than an explanation. Maybe this is why holy books are so filled with parables. Let me share this story with you:

> Two men, both seriously ill, occupied the same hospital room.
>
> One man was allowed to sit up in his bed for one hour each afternoon to help drain the fluid from his lungs. His bed was next to the room's only window.
>
> The other man had to spend all his time on his back. The two men talked for hours on end. They spoke of their wives and families, their homes, their jobs, their involvement in the military service, where they had been on vacation...
>
> Every afternoon, when the man by the window could sit up, he would pass the time by describing to his roommate the things he could see outside the window. The man in the other bed began to live for those one-hour periods where his world would be broadened and enlivened by all the activity and color of the world outside.

On Life

The window overlooked a park with a lovely lake. Ducks and swans played on the water while young children sailed their model boats. Young lovers walked arm in arm amid flowers of every color, and a fine view of the city skyline could be seen in the distance.

As the man by the window described all this in exquisite details, the man on the other side of the room would close his eyes and imagine the picturesque scene. One warm afternoon, the man by the window described a parade passing by. Although the other man could not hear the band, he could see it in his mind's eye as the gentleman by the window described it with descriptive words.

Days, weeks, and months passed. One morning the day nurse arrived to bring water for their baths, only to find the lifeless body of the man by the window, who had died peacefully in his sleep. She was saddened and called the hospital attendants to take the body away.

As soon as it seemed appropriate, the other man asked if he could be moved to the bed next to the window. The nurse was happy to make the switch, and after making sure he was comfortable, she left him alone.

Slowly, painfully, he propped himself up on one elbow to take his first look at the real world outside. He strained to slowly turn to look out the window beside the bed.

It faced a blank wall.

The man asked the nurse what could have compelled his deceased roommate, who had described such wonderful things outside his window.

The nurse responded that the man was blind and could not even see the wall. Perhaps he just wanted to encourage you and bring you joy.

The lesson to be learned here is that tremendous happiness can be had by making others happy, despite our own situations.

Everyone with whom you have contact should feel their life has been enriched because of their association with you.

> *"Just by changing your perspective on life, you can not only alter your own experiences, you can change the world."*
>
> Yongey Mingyur Rinpoche
> Teacher and Master of Tibetan Buddhism

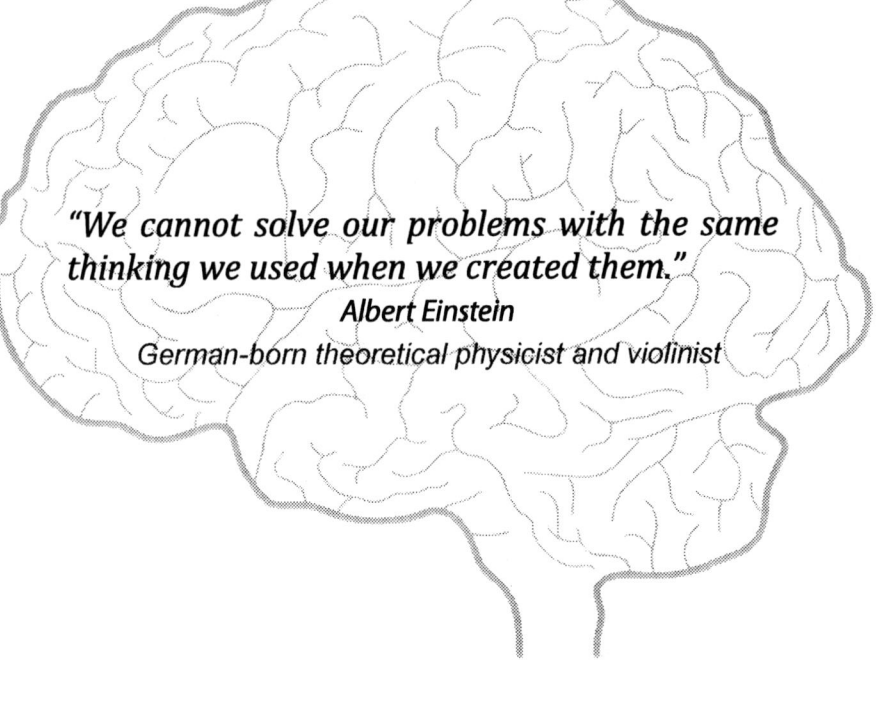

"We cannot solve our problems with the same thinking we used when we created them."
Albert Einstein
German-born theoretical physicist and violinist

COMMON SENSE MATTERS

On Life

Train Your Brain...Open up your mind and think

Be Inquisitive and Search: Innovative people spend twice as much time as their noninnovative counterparts searching for insights. Their calendars look very different. Always be asking questions. Always be meeting new and different people. People love to feel their opinions are meaningful and important. By asking questions of people, they will respond to you with a wealth of information. You can then edit out what you don't want or need and keep the gems that will help you grow. It is an art to know what questions to ask what people—**and the only way you can develop this art is by doing it all the time**. This way you learn what works and what does not work.

Know when to log off: Spending time on the web and social media can bring about "A-HA!" moments. But surfing Facebook, Twitter, or Pinterest is just one part of a balanced "thought" diet. Too much of this, however, and you run the risk of travelling the same well-worn paths over and over again. Ignore the pull that excessive social media can exert. Train your brain (by repetition) to move beyond the ruts you normally live in. **Remember, a rut is a grave with the ends knocked out.**

Facts are great and necessary, and friends' postings and idea-sharing are fun, but allow for some "unplugged" time—for your brain to be unfettered. Pursue ideas in other galaxies or universes. Open your mind and let your imagination soar!

> *"I like nonsense; it wakes up the brain cells. Fantasy is a necessary ingredient in living; it's a way of looking at life through the wrong end of a telescope. Which is what I do and it enables you to laugh at life's realities."*
> *Theodore "Doctor Seuss" Geisel*

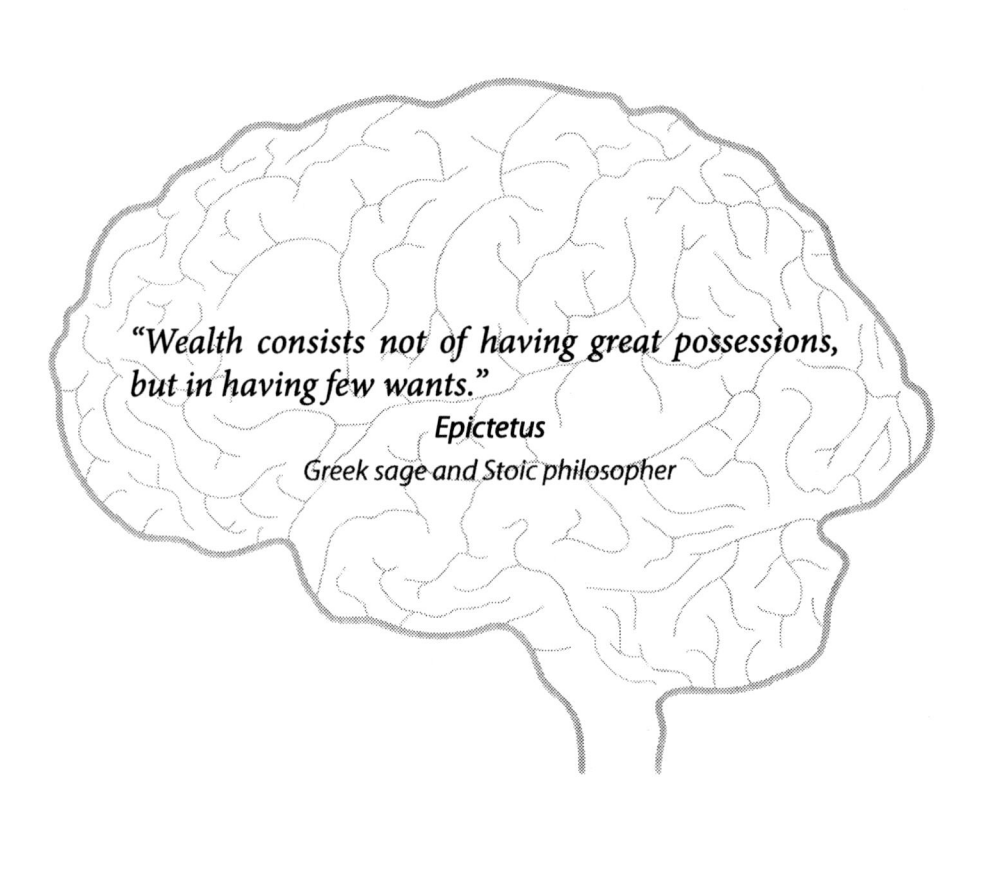

"Wealth consists not of having great possessions, but in having few wants."
Epictetus
Greek sage and Stoic philosopher

COMMON SENSE MATTERS

On Life

Financial and Emotional Wealth... *Take basic "Un-Common Sense" to achieve results*

At the outset, let me say there are numerous ways to create wealth. There is no one golden rule. Thousands of books have been written on this subject. However, you have a better chance at wealth if you adhere to certain principles. For starters, I suggest that everyone read the book *The Richest Man in Babylon* by George Clason. Principles laid out in this easy-to-read book will prove invaluable if you are looking for financial security.

Let's have a look at a few of my *truisms* for accumulating wealth:

- To achieve success, be neither an optimist nor a pessimist, but a realist with a hopeful nature.
- Count your blessings to enrich yourself and your neighbors—first spiritually, and then, financially.
- Focus on the positive, but do not ignore the negative.
- Always save a certain percentage of ANY money you receive, irrespective of your debt.
- When investing, be sure to spread your risk; invest in property, stocks, bonds, and mutual funds. Have a balanced portfolio.
- Always ensure you have at least six months living expenses in CASH.

- When investing, neither FEAR nor GREED is a good strategy.
- Let your money work for you, and remember that patience is a virtue.
- If you want to prosper, investigate before you invest.
- Looking out for Number One, doesn't make you Number One.

Review the statements listed below, and edit them to fit your personal situation:

- *I'm going to do the work I enjoy. You only live once, so do what you love.*
- *I will use* pull *whenever I can to open the doors to opportunity, but I will make sure to work with all my heart, body, and soul, once the door has been opened for me.*
- *I will recognize and be alert to my own weaknesses and find people to help me who excel in the things where I falter.*
- *I will consider an opportunity to advance more important than a mere financial gain.*
- *I will always stretch my abilities and goals a little further than my comfort zone.*
- *I will learn from my failures and then put them behind me.*
- *I will follow the Golden Rule. I will not engage in a transaction where someone else is shortchanged, cheated, or taken advantage of.*
- *I will use other people's money, provided I feel certain the money itself can grow at a faster rate than the interest charges.*
- *I will not be greedy.*

Develop a creed that will govern your approach to your life and your attitude.

> *I have always believed that to create real wealth, one must DREAM BIG. I did. That was why I started promoting boxing (at first, as a hobby that made as much money as my regular business). But it wasn't getting big enough, quickly enough. I lived in South Africa at the height of apartheid. I also had a political dream that I was to contribute in some small way to try and effect some change in that policy. My partners and I had an idea where we could combine two dreams into one and make one colossal statement. The apartheid policy had never allowed "mixed sports," i.e., a black sportsman could not compete against a white sportsman—in any sport. Well, after much negotiating with the government, we were allowed to promote fights that were "color blind." It was the first time in South African history this had happened. We were on our way. We created a crack (albeit small) in the apartheid policy, and we were now able to promote fights that were three or four times larger than before. We made money hand over fist, and promoted fights from the Palace in Monaco, with Prince Rainier and Princess Grace as hosts, to filling a 100,000-seat stadium in Pretoria.*

*You can create wealth at any level—
the bigger you think, the bigger the reward.*

Just use Common Sense.

"The clock is running. Make the most of today. Time waits for no man. Yesterday is history. Tomorrow is a mystery. Today is a gift. That's why it is called the present."
　　　　　Alice Morse Earle
　　　American historian & author,
　　　　Sun Dials and Roses of
　　　Yesterday: Garden Delights

COMMON SENSE MATTERS

On Life

Do It Now...Later is always too late

Procrastination—a thief of time. It steals from the value and essence of your personal and professional life. Why do people put things off? We could write a book on procrastination, but I'll try to sum it up in a couple of pages.

Procrastinators can have a fear of the future; underestimate their ability to get things done; not know what to do or how to do it; not thrive under pressure; set themselves up for failure; embrace disappointment; like being a victim; have too much on their plate; fail to set clear priorities; have poor time management skills; or be just plain lazy. Yet the biggest reason for procrastination **is the inability to pull the trigger—the inability to make a decision**. Don't decide not to decide. Make a decision and act on it. If it was the wrong decision—then make another one to correct the first decision.

Time is a finite resource. And this is another reason to "do it now." When you lose a minute doing nothing or thinking of something for the umpteenth time, you can never get that minute back. It is gone forever. This is one of the reasons I can't stand someone being late for an appointment. If you say 3:00, it does not mean 3:10. It is so disrespectful to take something finite away from a person that they can never get back. My wife always admonishes me for getting upset if I am kept waiting.

A couple of years ago I felt vindicated when I heard Sean Connery on a talk show. He told the interviewer that if he has an appointment for a specific time, and that person is not there exactly on time, he will not be there two minutes later. He went on to say he has no patience for people who disrespect his most precious commodity—time.

As I said earlier, time is finite. Don't waste a precious second of it, because once it is gone, it is gone forever. The clock is running; make the most of every second of every day.

To realize the value of one year, ask the student who failed a grade.
To realize the value of one month, ask the mother who gave birth to a premature baby.
To realize the value of one week, ask the editor of a weekly newspaper.
To realize the value of one hour, ask the lovers who are waiting to meet.
To realize the value of one minute, ask the person who just missed the train.
To realize the value of a second, ask the person who just avoided an accident.
To realize the value of one millisecond, ask the person who won a silver medal at the Olympics.

Respect time; refuse to waste it by procrastinating.

There can be a great cost to procrastination.

- Anxiety and frustration can lead to procrastination and indecision.
- You create stress through the anxiety and frustration by failing to make a decision, second guessing yourself on a continuous

basis when, in fact, that time could be spent doing something productive.
- *People who procrastinate and do not make decisions or don't "do it now" tend not to be respected and are very often viewed as being weak, and this can lead to......*
- *......failure, and......*
- *......increased anxiety and frustration.*

And this is **not** a formula for $ucce$$.

How many times have you said, "If only I would have..."? When opportunity knocks, open the door and invite her in, or she may not return. Opportunity is *La Belle Dame Sans Merci—a beautiful lady with no mercy.*

<u>Develop a Do-It-Now Philosophy</u>

I have observed losers in all walks of life. They tend to have several common traits. They all tend to...

- *Hope without conviction*
- *Dream without commitment*
- *Plan without action*
- *Scheme without substance*
- *Brag without performance*
- *Talk without ever getting started*

Winners are the opposite. They dream...they plan...they commit themselves...they take action...they make mistakes...they make another decision to put it right…they make another mistake…they make another decision to put it right…they have humility…and when all is said and done, their actions speak louder than their words ever could.

Time flies and won't return.
Work well, my friend, and learn.

Do it now!

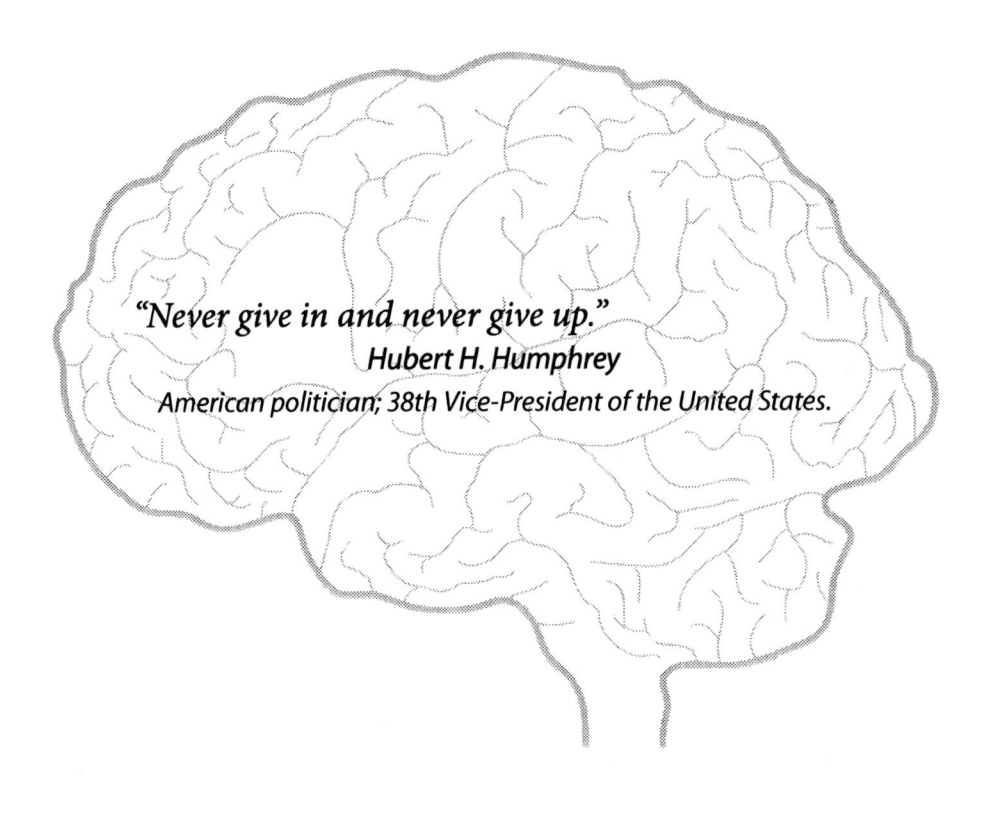

"Never give in and never give up."
Hubert H. Humphrey
American politician; 38th Vice-President of the United States.

COMMON SENSE MATTERS

On Life

Never Give Up... Ability will only get you so far

This is a subject that has been written about *ad nauseam*. I could cite hundreds—no, thousands—of examples of people who have "never given up" and have eventually come out on top. Some will reduce you to tears; others will make you want to stand on the coffee table and cheer. So instead of rehashing numerous stories like this, I want to focus on some facts about a prolific author, an unlikely intellectual, and arguably one of the greatest centers in basketball history. He is a member of the Basketball Hall of Fame, the NBA's all-time leading scorer. He won three national titles in college and six in the NBA.

Paramount among all the lessons one can learn from Kareem Abdul-Jabbar's career is that no matter how talented you are in any field of work, be humble and be willing to listen and learn.

> At thirty-eight years of age, Kareem Abdul-Jabbar, captain of the Los Angeles Lakers, was nearing the end of his Hall of Fame career. Then came NBA's Memorial Day Massacre in 1985. In the first game of the NBA Play-offs, the Lakers were smothered, 148 to 114, by Larry Bird, Kevin McHale, Robert Parish and rest of the Boston Celtics. Abdul-Jabbar had only contributed twelve points and three rebounds. People wrote him off. In the three days before the return match, he worked on every aspect of

his game—and in his own words—<u>particularly on his mental approach</u>. He went personally to each and every teammate, apologized for his poor performance in the previous game, and made a contract with them that it would never happen again. At thirty-eight, he is reported to have put in more work than any of the younger members of his team; he drove himself, hour after hour, day after day. In the second game of the series against the Celtics, he went on to score thirty points and had seventeen rebounds. The Lakers won 109-102. In game three, Abdul-Jabbar became the league's all-time, leading, play-off scorer. And after the Lakers won the title in six games, Kareem Abdul-Jabbar was named MVP of the Finals.

The attributes that make a Hall of Famer in life, as well as in sport, are the same intangible instincts that make you realize talent and hard work will only get you so far. You need that inner fortitude that will never let you give up and drive you always to be improving. It must come from your heart and gut.

***Never take anything for granted,
no matter how talented you are...
and never stop working hard!***

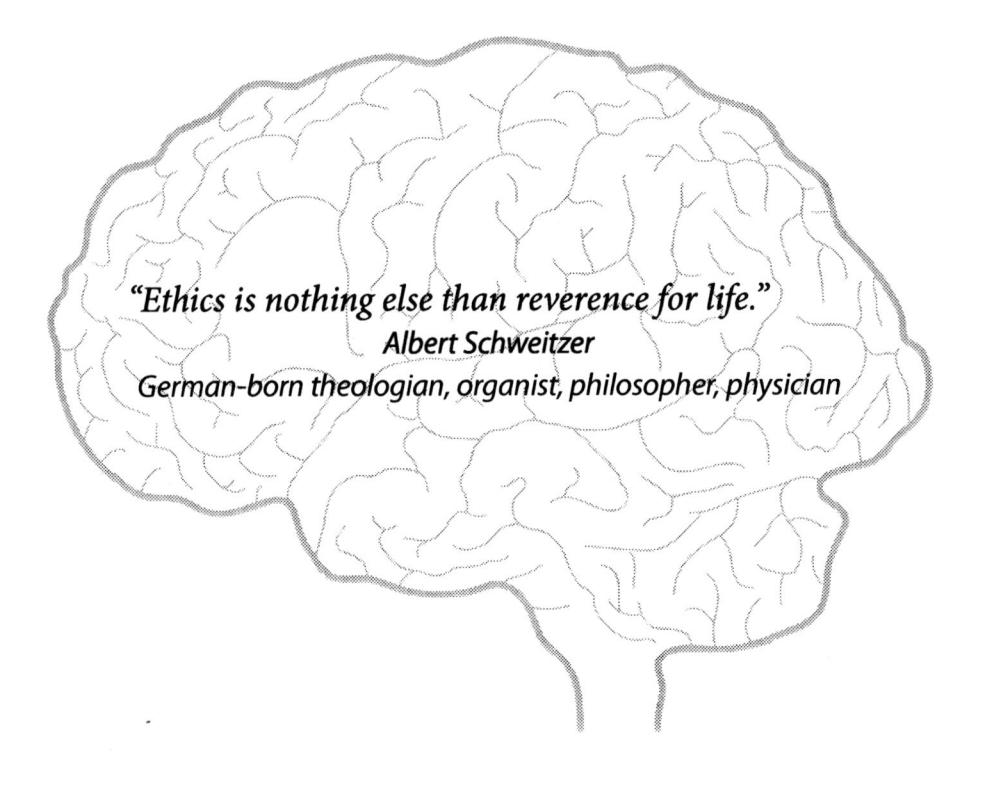

"Ethics is nothing else than reverence for life."
Albert Schweitzer
German-born theologian, organist, philosopher, physician

COMMON SENSE MATTERS

On Life

The Ethics of Excellence...*Never compromise your Personal Value System*

If you were to look in the dictionary to see their definition of "ethics," you would find, "That branch of philosophy dealing with values related to human conduct, with respect to the 'rightness' and 'wrongness' of certain actions, and to the 'goodness' and 'badness' of the motives and ends of such actions."

But, you see, in the real world we have a problem in determining what may be, or what may not be ethical—principally because what is ethical to one person may not be ethical to another. One person may say it is ethical to tell a little white lie to spare someone's feelings. Another person may say, "A lie is a lie, no matter the color." One person may say it is OK to steal from the rich if the spoils go to the poor. Another person may say, "Stealing is wrong, no matter what you do with the spoils." How many times have we heard it said, "All is fair in love and war"?

These are not questions to be answered here because in so many instances an action that one person may feel is ethical is considered by another to be unethical. Let me tell you how I handle this: When you are questioning yourself about whether an action you are about to take is ethical or not, visualize God standing in front of you. You are looking into His face, and He into yours. Then, if you would be proud to do what you were questioning, it will be ethical. If not, well…

- Let your character be revealed in the small stuff, so others come to see you, and you come to see yourself, as one who acts ethically in all things.
- Any violation of honesty and integrity, however small, dilutes your ethical strength, leaving you weaker for the big challenges you are bound to face.
- Don't allow your finer instincts to become a casualty of the little everyday crimes of ethical compromise.

Integrity, honesty, and compassion—leaders always talk about the value of these character traits. They will always tell you their greatest concern is to hold a very high ethical and moral standard. You can build this core standard the same way you can build muscles in a gym. Workers who exercise good character feel better about their accomplishments and themselves.

> *A good rule of thumb about ethics…if you have to question the ethics of an action you are about to take, it is probably the wrong thing to do.*

"All coaching is, is taking a player where he can't take himself."
  Bill McCartney
  University of Colorado Head Football Coach
  Founder of Promise Keepers Men's Ministry

COMMON SENSE MATTERS

On Life

On Coaching... Always HAVE a coach and BE a coach to others

Understand that on the journey through life, no man is an island—we all need counsel and advice.

Have a Coach... *Irrespective of your Experience or Age*

The thing that I regret most in life is that, in my formative years, I never had a coach or a mentor. Around the age of fifty, I found a solution to this void, which I will discuss with you shortly—but I sincerely believe that from the youngest age, everyone needs a person, or people, who they can look up to, go to for guidance—someone who will be able to give them advice through the spectrum of their personal and professional life.

There comes a time when growing up that a child realizes that their parents are not the Almighty incarnate. They are human and, consequently, fallible. Very often, the void that realization creates is filled by a grandparent, or maybe a sports coach. But in the grand scheme of things, this relationship does not last forever, either. Many people turn to their priest or rabbi—great for spiritual guidance but maybe not much else. Others may turn to a therapist—and there is a place for a therapist in many lives. But I am talking about someone whose counsel you are not using "professionally," but rather someone who is there for you because they care. As a person matures, they need to find someone they can look up to, who can give them guidance, advice, and counsel, as well as be a friend who offers comfort and solace when needed. Sometimes this may not be a single person but a select few. What very often happens is the more successful a person is in life (invariably this success is measured in dollars), the less they believe they need a mentor. Ego, pride, and maybe embarrassment get in the way. This type of person may be financially successful but will not maximize their wisdom.

Let me tell you how I learned this, and then you can take the basic principle and adapt it to your own set of circumstances:

> *I had a friend back in South Africa by the name of Stan who was an excellent insurance salesman. He was a member of the Million Dollar Club (forty years ago), yet he was always broke. He couldn't manage his business or his money. This really stressed him out, and he came to me for advice. After much discussion and brain storming, we came up with a plan. He was going to invite three people he respected to be part of a group he would put together. Each one would have a special talent they brought to the table. He invited a banker, a casual associate who not only understood the banking world but also had common sense. He invited an attorney who was a friend of a friend but was known to be a hard, straight-talking man. And he invited me, and my credential was that I had a lot of business experience in building successful companies. This was the deal: He wanted to meet the three of us for lunch once a month for an hour. He would pay us for our time. Our charge was to give him professional advice—AND TO HOLD HIS FEET TO THE*

> FIRE, TO DO WHAT WE TOLD HIM TO DO. This was Stan's personal board of directors, so to speak. He took our advice. We challenged him continuously. He listened and followed through on his assignments (he was committed)—in five years he was a millionaire!!! In currency of forty years ago, when a million bucks was a million bucks.

Now, I challenge you to take this model and tailor it to fit your life, your set of circumstances. Your board can be one person or ten. The person can be older or younger than you (I have learned more from my son than any other person I know)—just pick the right team.

Ask your mentor(s) or coach whether you are holding yourself accountable. Get a 360-degree feedback from coworkers, vendors, customers. You will be surprised how much you will learn about yourself, whether you run a multimillion-dollar corporation or whether you are a regular nice person in a regular nice position in a regular nice company.

Have a Coach…Irrespective of your experience or age

A trainer is…

…one who trains an athlete, an animal, a racehorse, to **physically** compete against competition. In some instances, the competition may be a stop watch, a team, or an individual. They are trained to be fitter, stronger, and more able to meet the demands of whatever activity they may be entered in.

A coach is…

…one who develops a strategy that enables people to meet their goals for improved performance and career enhancement by **thinking and**

planning correctly to be smarter and more mentally prepared to meet the challenges of competition.

One cannot coach a dog to do tricks, or a racehorse to run a strategic race—but one can train them. The difference here is verbal explanation is needed to coach, just as much as intellect is needed to understand coaching. Consequently, a coaching approach is needed to maximize a person's potential.

This definition differs from the model some of us bring from some athletic activities: an authority figure telling people what to do differently. In truth, the focus should be on the "coached" rather than the coach. The assumption is that the coached has a goal that the coach helps him/her meet. The relationship involves a two-way dialog, as opposed to the one-way telling (which is most common in training). Also, the focus is positive and objective, focusing on particular improvements that the coach and the coached want to achieve, rather than on physical deficiencies or shortcomings.

Be a Coach...Help others be better than they can be alone

Great coaches build winners on the strength of their natural talents. Take the scenario of Golfer Joe, who goes to a pro for lessons. The coach could teach him to grip the club like Tiger Woods. He could teach him to swing like Tiger Woods. He could teach him to follow through like Tiger Woods. But Golfer Joe will never be able to play like Tiger Woods. A good coach takes the natural talent of Golfer Joe and builds on that to make him the best he can be. He will be "Joe the First" instead of "Tiger the Second." Great coaches build winners on the natural talents of their students *in any walk of life*.

You see that the one thing that Tiger Woods does that no one can imitate is how he thinks when he is standing over a six foot putt to win $1,000,000. <u>A good coach teaches his student how to think in a way that fits his personality and temperament.</u> It doesn't matter how the student (Joe) copies the physical attributes another person (Tiger), if he does not have the right mental approach, he will never have the same results as Tiger.

On the human side:

> *Throughout life you must get the input of others.*
> *Throughout your life you must*
> *hold yourself accountable.*
> *Throughout your life you must be measured.*

> *"It is in your moments of decision that your destiny is shaped."*
>
> **Tony Robbins**
> *American life coach, self-help author & motivational speaker*

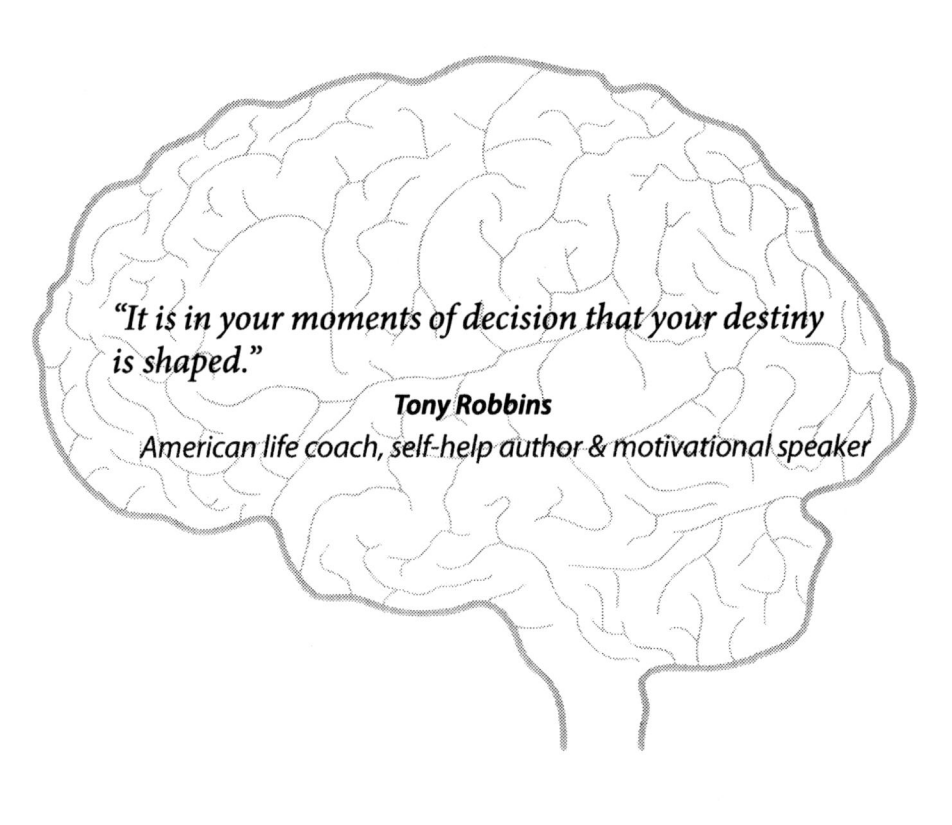

COMMON SENSE MATTERS

On Life

Choose wisely... Your life is a result of the choices you make

Nearly every moment of our lives we make decisions. Some are life changing, while others seem insignificant at the time. All choices lead to consequences. Some are positive and some are negative. We always have options and choices. We may not like some of them, but we always have them.

Each of us must take personal responsibility for the quality of our life. To point the finger at anyone other than yourself for your life's outcome is to live in frustration and denial. Each of us is free to choose any path. **Choose wisely, for tomorrow's harvest is planted today**.

What consequences are you paying today as a result of past choices? If you could go back in time with what you know now, would you have made different choices? If so, what would you have wanted the new outcome to be?

It is interesting to note that people who are happy understand that they made the best choices they could, with the information, experience, and insight that was available to them at the time—even if the result was not as expected.

On Life

Here is a choice I didn't like making. My parents did not want me to marry the girl that I was in love with. In fact, they gave me the BIG ultimatum!! I had to make a choice between my parents and the woman I loved. Well, the decision I made was to follow my heart, so my sweetheart and I came to America to get married. We ultimately had to return to South Africa (because of immigration laws) but made it back to the United States twenty-one years later. Today, we have been married for well over fifty years. My parents eventually came 'round in the end, so it was a good choice.

The choices we are given present us with the opportunity to move steadily in the direction of a better way of life as we move toward our destiny—just like our decision to live in America. If we choose wisely, we move smoothly toward this destination. If we choose poorly, we are guided back to the correct path.

When making choices, always keep in mind the long-term ramifications. Project yourself ahead and ask yourself if you were looking back on today, would you be happy with the decision you just made.

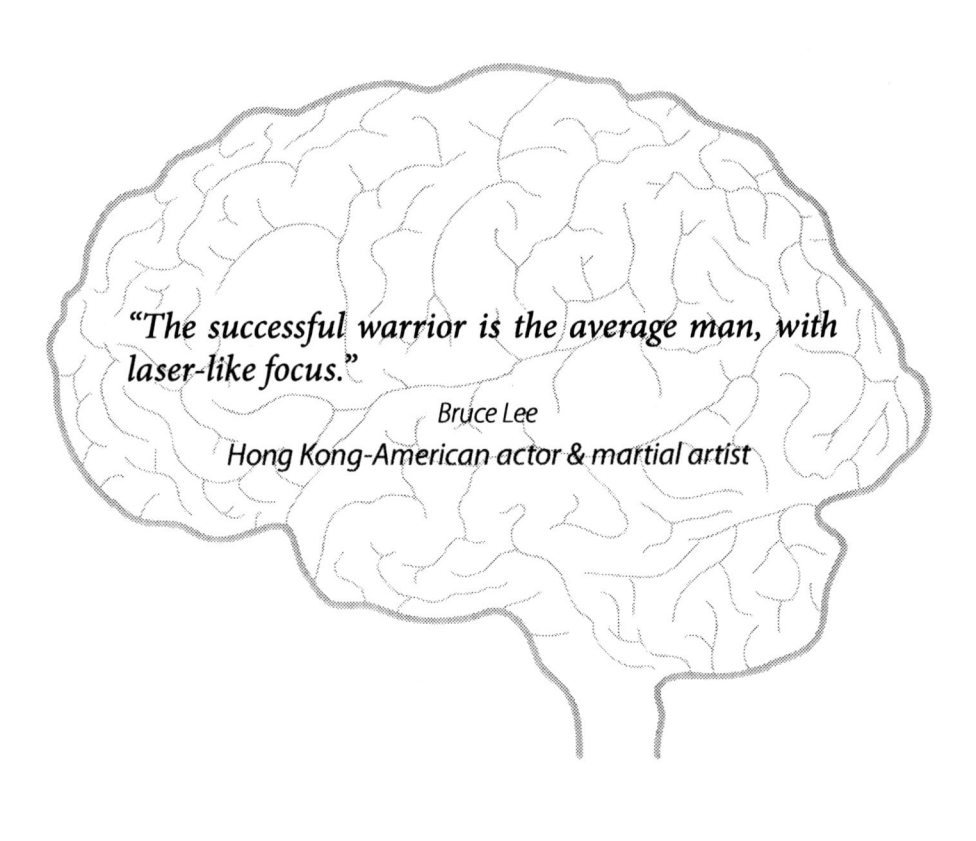

"The successful warrior is the average man, with laser-like focus."

Bruce Lee
Hong Kong-American actor & martial artist

COMMON SENSE MATTERS

On Life

*Focus Your Time...*on the important, not the urgent

We have all heard the adage, "Q. How do you eat a 2,000 pound elephant?...A. *One bite at a time.*" Well, the same principle should be applied when we are applying our focus to our time. For instance, don't think of the year. Break it down into months. Don't think of months. Break it down into weeks. Don't think of weeks. Break it down into days or hours. This principle will enable you focus, as opposed to always viewing the big picture.

Invest your time wisely: Our lives are a result of how we invest our time. Good health requires us to invest hours in sleep, exercise, and eating properly. Likewise, a career requires time for strategic planning, honing skills, networking, and dreaming up new ideas. Too much of our time is wasted on meaningless activities. ***Time is a nonrenewable resource. Even the best of us are only allocated twenty-four hours a day.***

Play to your strengths, as your time is limited: Boost what makes the most difference to you here and now. Tomorrow is a blank slate. Play offense and make things happen. Don't wait for things to happen. **Do the *important* things first—not the *urgent* (which may be trivial),**

because if your *important* thing becomes *urgent*…you will have a <u>*crisis*</u> **on your hands.**

Plan: Where do you want to be one week, one month, one year, five years from now? Then break it down into small steps, and FOCUS on these steps in the knowledge that **by doing this you will reach your goal.**

Rank your steps: When you have broken down the steps you need to achieve a specific task or goal, prioritize them. Then work on the top priority without shifting your focus to number TWO until number ONE is complete. This will allow you to focus totally on this activity without wasting nervous energy on other tasks. **Because of this total focus your task will be completed sooner, which will earn you more time for other activities.**

Pick your battles carefully: This all being said, avoid unjustified perfection, so you don't get bogged down overdoing things that will not give you a good return on your time investment.

Ranking priorities and planning tasks are necessary steps for focus and successful time management. But beware of *over planning*, as this can lead to *analysis paralysis*. Then the only *thing* that gets done is no*thing*.

It is better to be 80 percent right "now,"
rather than 100 percent right "never!"

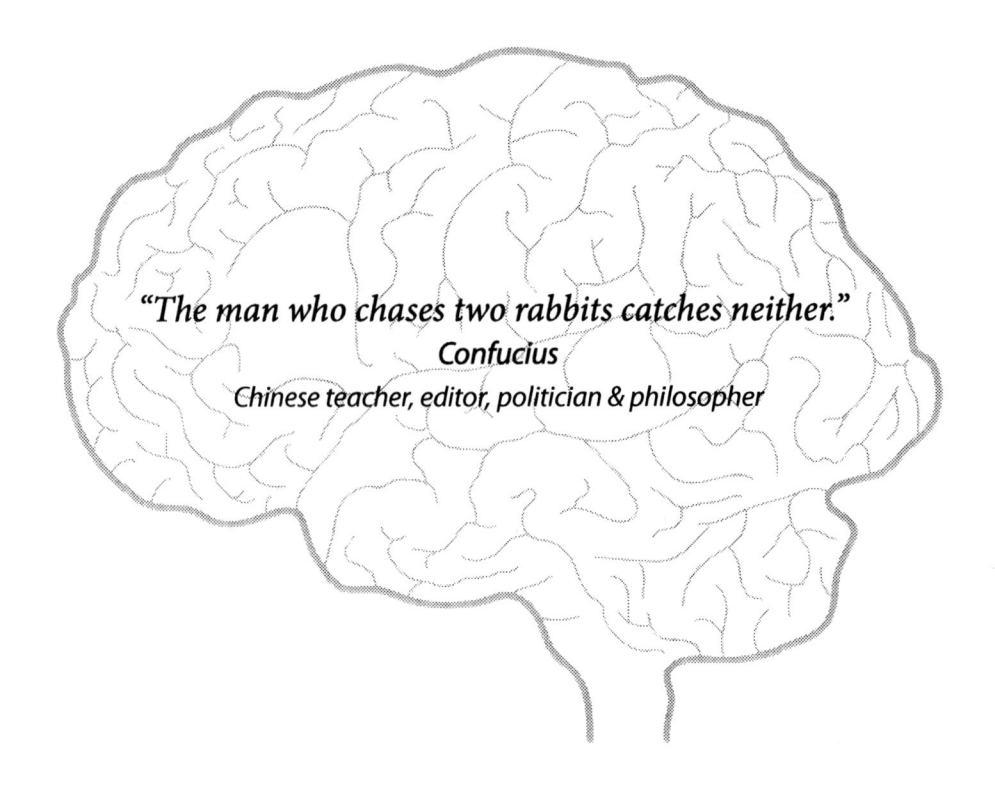

> *"The man who chases two rabbits catches neither."*
> *Confucius*
> *Chinese teacher, editor, politician & philosopher*

COMMON SENSE MATTERS

On Life

Focus... *How do you know you've arrived if you didn't know where you were going in the first place?*

You tend to bring into your life that which is consistent with your focus. You can either focus on what is not working or what is working; what you don't have or what you do have; what you don't want or what you want; what you don't believe in or what you do believe in. Remember, don't waste precious time focusing on things you have no control over. There is a great old adage that applies here: **"Be careful what you ask for, you just might get it."**

Focus means having such pinpointed concentration that you allow nothing to interfere with the process. It is not allowing yourself to become sidetracked while you are trying to achieve a goal. To truly focus is not easy.

Losers in life focus on what is missing, where they are not, and what they can't do. Winners in life are grateful for their blessings and focus on what they want, have, and can do. Losers invariably focus on the reasons they cannot succeed at a goal or a task. They always blame an "outside influence" that prevents them from achieving a specific goal or task. Winners, on the other hand, learn to work with what they have. They improvise, innovate, adjust, compromise—**whatever it takes to get the job done, with the tools they have.**

On Life

Arguably the greatest heavyweight boxer that ever lived was Rocky Marciano. He had forty-nine fights and never lost one—and he only weighed 195 lbs. In his bid for the world title against Jersey Joe Walcott, he was taking a real hammering throughout the entire fight (in fact he was knocked down in the first round) but would not take a step back. At the end of the twelfth round, with only three rounds to go—and being behind on all the judges' scorecards—he told his trainer (Al Weill) he thought he was at "the gates of hell" because of the pain in his chest (he had two broken ribs) and that his arms felt like lead—and he added he was blind and couldn't see a thing, as both eyes were so swollen and bloodied. He asked Al to throw in the towel. His trainer then asked if he could see him standing in front of him. Rocky's answer was, "Yes, but you are only a dim blur." Al then asked him if he remembered that so far he was the only man in heavyweight history who had never been beaten. "Yes," was his response. His trainer then said (and I am paraphrasing), "Take all the pain you have and put it aside. You are not allowed to think about it. When you stand up, there will be a blur in front of you. It will be Jersey Joe coming in for the kill. Don't think of anything other than the round lasts 180 seconds, you will throw 200 punches at that blur and be the greatest heavyweight in history. Total focus." Rocky did just that. He knocked Jersey Joe into a stupor in the thirteenth round. When Jersey Joe was draped over the ropes, out cold, Rocky was still throwing punches because he didn't realize Jersey Joe wasn't standing any longer. Rocky's trainer had to go into the ring to get him because he couldn't find his corner. Both fighters spent the next few days in hospital. I often wonder if Mr. Stallone modeled his "Rocky" on Mr. Marciano.

Fast forward. When I met Rocky in South Africa about a month before he died in a plane crash, I asked him about this fight. He told me that during that last round he was so focused on swinging a punch every second at the blur in front of him, he never felt the pain in his broken ribs and leaden arms. Now, my friends, THIS IS FOCUS.

In life, when you have set a goal, whether it is business or personal, make sure that you have this pinpoint focus. *Let nothing distract you.* Be resolute in focusing on the end result you are aiming to achieve.

> **F**or
> **O**ur
> **C**ontinued
> **U**nlimited
> **$**ucce**$$**

A key ingredient in all leaders, winners, effective people, and productive, successful organizations is: FOCUS. What is your focus today? Is it a focus on a positive outcome?

Focus on your goal; it is your destination and your destiny.
When you attain it you will know you have arrived.

"The more you praise and celebrate your life, the more there is to celebrate."
Oprah Winfrey
American media proprietor, talk show host, actress, producer, and philanthropist

COMMON SENSE MATTERS

On Life

Celebrate Victories…*Embrace the rewards*

There is very little in life that gives a person more pleasure than winning. Which Wimbledon champion didn't throw themselves on the grass after winning the final point in the fifth set? How many golfers do you see pumping their fists when they sink a long putt? Think of taking your significant other to dinner because you won the sales competition at the office, or giving your kid a *high five* when she got an A on her math test. These are all celebrations. Every victory, grand or small, deserves a celebration.

Don't be shy about celebrating your victories. Stand on the highest mountain and express yourself in any way you feel appropriate that makes you feel good. When you feel good you will remember that feeling. It will become embedded in your subconscious. And you will want to experience that feeling again, and again…and again…and again. This will drive you and motivate you to win at something again, and again…and again…(you get the message). Have you ever wondered why so many people seem to win nearly all the time? They are driven to win by wanting to feel that exaltation of winning the prize or pumping their fist—just one more time. My, how I celebrated when I won my club's singles tennis title for the fifth consecutive time. It felt so good I just had to do it again…and did.

On Life

In working with a large, Florida-based distributor of swimming pool supplies, we had one year when we beat the highest sales record the company had ever achieved. We took every manager—and a few support people that contributed to our success—and their significant others to New York for a few days. We did the whole "nine yards." The best restaurants—Broadway shows—shopping…we did it all. But most important of all, we took the Saturday morning, sat in the board room of the hotel, and "got to know each other." We all told a story about our lives that no one in the room knew about us. When we finished, there was not a dry eye in the house. We laughed; we cried. Many friendships were formed that day; the rest were solidified. The celebration of success paid many dividends. It motivated the managers to want a similar celebration the next year, and the next year, and the next year. We celebrated from the Napa Valley, through Las Vegas, and back to the East Coast. Stronger friendships were forged and team spirit—which is the backbone of HornerXpress (and that of any successful company)—was made even stronger.

My friends, when you win—no matter how small the victory may be—savor it and celebrate it.

Program your subconscious to know that the reward for winning is a celebration!

COMMON SENSE MATTERS

ON LEADING

"I must follow the people. Am I not their leader?"

Benjamin Disraeli
British Conservative politician, writer and aristocrat and twice Prime Minister

"Common sense is the thing a horse has which keeps him from betting on people."
W. C. Fields
American comedian, actor, juggler and writer

COMMON SENSE MATTERS

A Common Sense Observation on Leading

Leading covers a vast array of roles. Parents are leaders. Pastors and choir directors are leaders. There are leaders of large corporations and leaders of average and small companies. There are department heads and divisional managers in a variety of different-sized businesses who are all leaders. Sometimes a leader may be appointed for a single project.

We all have relationships with leaders; either we are one, we follow one (maybe both), or we are married to one!

Young people, in business and in life, can learn leadership skills simply by recognizing and understanding what it takes to be a good leader IF they have the talent for it.

So, when reading the pages that follow, not all the situations may apply to you here and now. But I am sure that at some time in your life, you will experience the challenges and have to exercise the skill sets necessary to be a good leader.

Use your "Common Sense" to recognize which situations may apply to you here and now to enhance your current leadership role.

COMMON SENSE MATTERS

Index of Thoughts on Leading

Principles of Leadership... Lead by actions...not by words 113
Win Trust With Honor... Lead as you would want to be led 119
Understanding the Importance of Change... The only constant in life is change.. 123
Hiring Smart... Surround yourself with people who can "do it better" than you.. 129
A Roadmap to Success... Plan from the top down—and work from the bottom up 137
Communicate... Speak in conversation, not monologue 143
Be Open with Employees... They want authenticity, not perfection, in their leaders... 149
Take Time to Think... Ready, AIM, fire" always works best!................. 153
Trim the Fat... Always run your business as if times are tough................ 157
Incentivize and Motivate... Use honey; not a big stick........................... 161
Inspire Your Organization... The worst mistake a boss can make is to not say, "well done.".. 165
It is Not a Sale Until the Cash is in the Bank... Profit is not profit on paper alone. 169
Measure Everything... You can't manage it if you don't measure it 175
Create a Competitive Advantage... Play to your strengths 179
Why Leaders Fail... Keep your eye on the "right" ball............................ 183
Leadership is Not for Everyone... Step aside if you cannot step up. 191

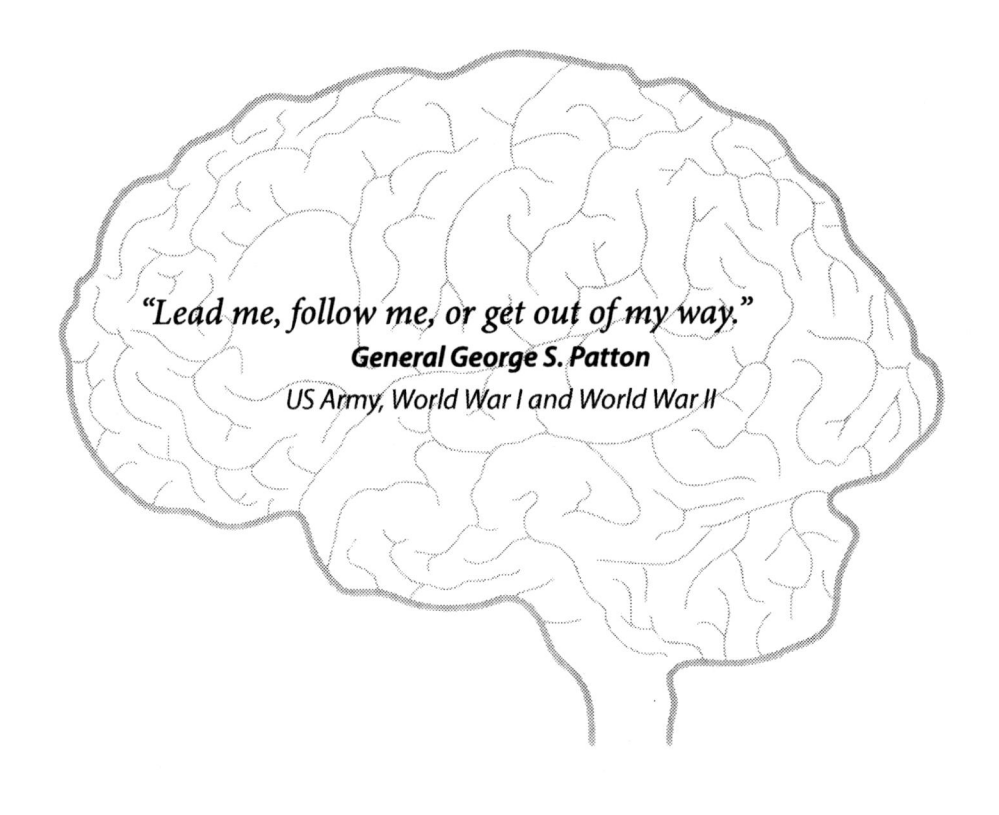

> *"Lead me, follow me, or get out of my way."*
> **General George S. Patton**
> *US Army, World War I and World War II*

COMMON SENSE MATTERS

On Leading

Principles of Leadership...Lead by actions...not only words

A strong leader has cultivated the wisdom and strength to know...

1. **The truth** cannot be compromised.
   In business you have numerous partners; there are stockholders, employees, customers, and vendors. The health of your business, to a greater or lesser degree, lies in the hands of each of these groups. As a leader of your company (or division, branch, etc.) they will take their lead from you. If you compromise the truth, they will believe it is acceptable to you, so they will return the compliment, which means you will never be maximizing your relationships with them. Truth <u>cannot</u> and <u>must not</u> be compromised.

2. **When you are wrong or fail**—admit it.
   If you have red blood in your veins, if your heart beats, if you get out of bed in the morning—you make mistakes. Everyone does. One of the greatest assets you can have in life is the respect of the people with whom you associate. You earn this respect by admitting you are human and make mistakes (irrespective of the title on your office door), and you also fail from time to time. When this happens, 'fess up. Admit it! Say, "I was wrong!

Let's make another decision, to right that wrong." Once again, this is an example your staff and associates will follow as well. They will learn from you that it's OK to be wrong, and (unless it becomes a habit) jobs are not in jeopardy.

3. **A company's two greatest assets**—its **people** and its **flexibility.**
   I keep stressing the most important ingredient any company can have is "A" people. It goes without saying that you cannot have an "A" organization with "B" people. But the second greatest asset a company can have is the ability to be flexible—its ability to change course quickly in this ever-changing world in which we live. What is right today may be wrong tomorrow, and vice versa. Be agents of change. Keep updating. Keep finding new ways to do old things.

4. **Be prepared to eat your own cooking.**
   When your actions result in a consequence for your staff, your vendors, or your customers, make sure that you would be prepared to accept the same consequence for yourself.

5. **Train for a sprint and a marathon.**
   Leaders must have the ability to act quickly and make snap decisions, as well as to plan for the long term. Too many leaders say, "Being in business is a marathon, not a sprint." Forget it! For a business leader, it is both.

6. **Believe in a lean and disciplined organization.**
   If your staff know their jobs, are well trained, and are self-disciplined, you will be able to have a lean, profitable company. Always run your company as you would want it to look to a

prospective buyer. As British Prime Minister Margaret Thatcher famously advised, "Disciplining yourself to do what you know is right and important, although difficult, is the high road to pride, self-esteem, and personal satisfaction."

7. **There are no friendly competitors.**
    You may be friends with a competitor at an association meeting. You may be friendly with a competitor on a casual basis—but please know that when all the chips are on the table and push comes to shove, they are in the *game of business* to win. And in order to survive, that must also be your position. At all times, maintain your integrity and ethics, but we live in a world of survival of the fittest, so recognize your competitors' goal is to win—which means they want to beat you—which in turn means they are not "friendly."

8. **Always strive** for increased market share.
    We all know that when the tide comes in, all the boats rise. When economic times are good, it is natural, to some extent, that sales will increase. However, some businesses may experience a 5 percent increase in business and believe they should be happy. Well, if that sector of the economy is experiencing a 7 percent increase, then that company is losing 2 percent market share. Unhealthy, to say the least. Always try to measure market share, in both up and down markets.

9. **Those who produce more** should share more.
    As Ichak Adizes points out in his book, *The Life Cycle of a Business*, every business, depending where it is in its growth cycle, has a certain *vitamin* that should run the company. There is vitamin "P," which is the Producer, normally the CEO at a business's

inception. There is the vitamin "A," which is the Administration (by the way, an accountant or attorney should never run a business). Then we have an "E," the Entrepreneur, and an "I," the Integrator. Companies in their prime should always be run by either of these two vitamins. I fully understand the concept of *team* and subscribe to it. However, the distribution of the "spoils" should not be equal. There should be a healthy percentage of profits set aside for employees that do not produce profits but keep the company machine well oiled. Then for those that produce profits (it may be a factory manager who improves efficiency, or a salesperson who sells at higher margins), there should be a benefit, in direct proportion to their contribution of profit. Every owner or stockholder is in business for profit. Those that contribute most should benefit most. Compensation and promotion should never be influenced by an employee's belief, tenure, gender, race, or friendship. This is not always easy to do, but who ever said being a great leader was easy?

10. **Be an opportunity seeker, not an entitlement taker.**
    True leaders look for opportunities to grow their companies. They are not focused on self-entitlement. For example, my son-in-law owns and operates a very large company. A few years into the company's successful operation, he purchased a used Volvo. When the company was a multi-million-dollar business, he upgraded his vehicle only because his staff nagged him to do so. How's that for not being an *entitlement taker*. When you think about this action, can you imagine how much respect he earned from the employees?

11. **Plan for succession.**
    Succession can mean either preparing your company to be a saleable entity that will net you enough cash to either retire or to enter your second career, or it can mean having the right people in the right places, properly trained, within your organization to enable you to step back without so much as a hiccup in the organization.

12. **Be mindful of your impact.**
    We have all been created in God's image, and the results of our leadership will be measured beyond the workplace. Your story will be told in the way you influence peoples' lives—make sure it is positively.

People first; strategy second

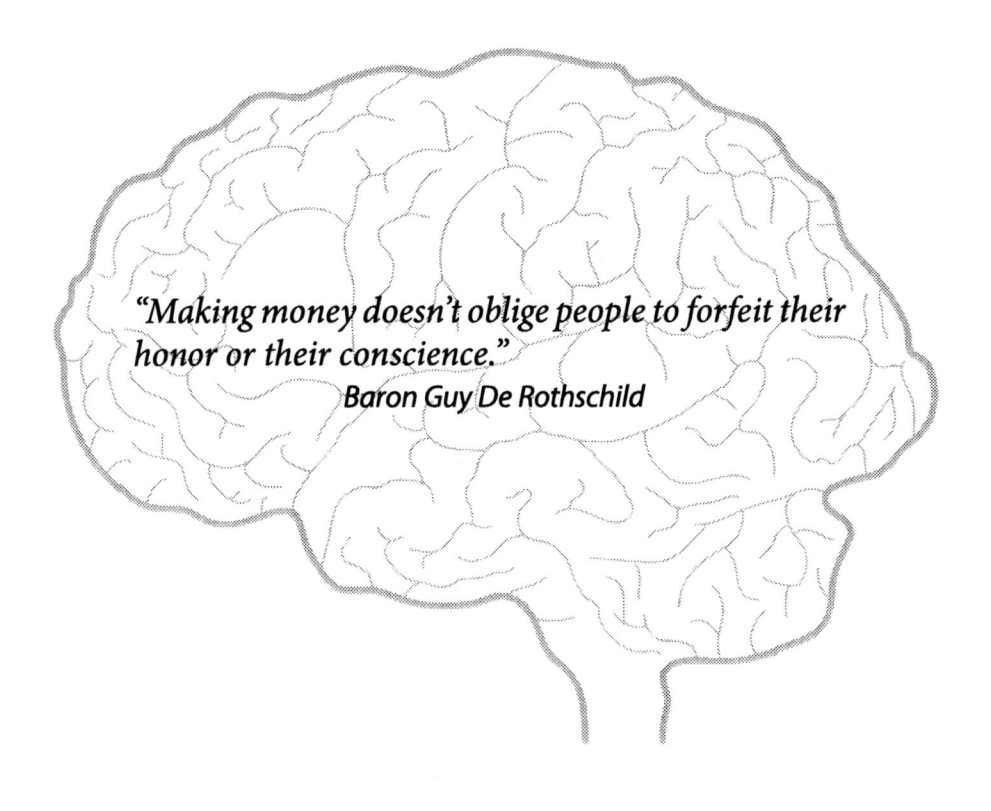

"Making money doesn't oblige people to forfeit their honor or their conscience."
Baron Guy De Rothschild

COMMON SENSE MATTERS

On Leading

Win Trust With Honor...*Lead as you would want to be led*

In a June 7, 2012, interview with Steve Watkins of the *Investor's Business Daily*, Chris McGoff, author of *The Primes*, said, "Integrity is little more than simply saying what you're going to do, then doing what you said. Trust is a function of promises being made and kept."

Legendary entrepreneur Warren Buffet says, "Trust is like the air we breathe. When it is present nobody notices it. But when it is absent everybody notices."

It's all too easy to compromise your principles to get that first deal, obtain financing, hire the people you want, or delay a promised payment, but in the end those decisions can destroy your business. The first step to having an ethical organization is for you to be a model of ethical behavior yourself. If your employees see you constantly cutting corners and working in gray areas, they are probably going to do the same thing, irrespective of what your written code of ethics may say. It is a monkey-see, monkey-do world we live in, and like it or not, you're the big monkey everyone looks up to in your company. This not only applies to CEO's but also to managers of corporate divisions or depaertments.

Ethical considerations pop up everywhere you look. Take technology. You could commit to buying software for every workstation in your company, instead of downloading the same piece of software into multiple machines, without paying for the right to do so. It is a common practice. It is also theft. Or you could create a policy of banning the use of bootlegged software, photos and other images, sound clips, and other material from the Internet, and refuse to engage in unethical spamming.

Let me share with you two areas of ethical focus:

CUSTOMERS: Every successful business should offer excellent customer service. No misleading claims. No promises not kept. No inferior products, etc. If a business reneges on these promises, customers will leave and tell others. And bad news travels at the speed of light.

EMPLOYEES: Pay them fairly. Don't treat them like third-class citizens. Include them in the decision-making process. Happy employees are productive. You will experience less turnover, which is a great cost saver in the long run.

Ask yourself the question, "Do I want ethics to be a random walk in the park, or do I want it be an intentional *foundation* of my business?"

Make ethics a top value in your life and people will trust you. There should never be a question in your mind as to whether the action you are taking is ethical or nor not. If you need to ask yourself that question, it is probably unethical. So, simply don't do it.

> One of the first examples I had of ethical thinking and action in business was when I was very young and working for a clothing

company as a salesperson. I got an order from the largest chain of departmental stores in the city. The order was for 1,000 dozen flannel pajamas. We made these PJs, and they were a hit, not only for our customer, but for our small factory as well. It kept our machines busy for the winter season, which was great, as we lived in a tropical climate, similar to Florida.

We got repeat orders for three consecutive years. In the fourth year, the Japanese manufacturer of the flannel sent us an inferior quality flannel. We had already paid for it. We knew if we made the PJs in this material and delivered them, they would be returned. But if we did not make and deliver the product, we would not have the cash to carry us through the winter—and this would cause dire consequences. It may have even caused us to close down. I remember upper management arguing about how to handle the problem—when the owner of the company stepped in and said there was only one way to handle the problem. He promptly took himself down to the head office of our customer and discussed it with their buying department, laying all his cards on the table. The end result was that the customer was so impressed by the honesty and integrity of my boss that they helped our company financially to get through the winter—and increased their business with us to the extent that we nearly doubled our size in two years.

"The measure of a man's real character is what he would do if he knew he would never be found out."
Thomas Macaulay
English historian, statesman

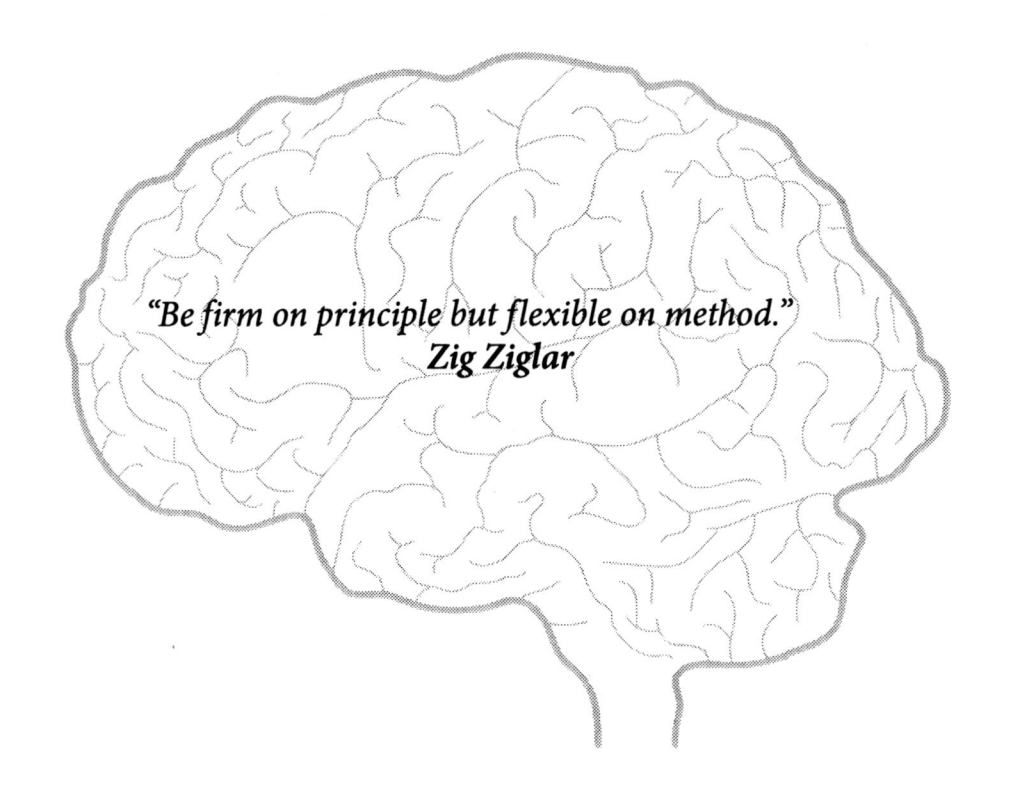

"Be firm on principle but flexible on method."
Zig Ziglar

COMMON SENSE MATTERS

On Leading

Understanding the Importance of Change...
The only constant in life is change

Ichak Adizes, the author of the best seller *Managing Corporate Lifecycles* points out, quite correctly, that the greatest asset a business can have is *flexibility*. In this fast-moving world, without the ability to be flexible in our thoughts and processes, we are doomed to mediocrity.
In 1995 I gave a talk to the National Tooling and Machine Association. I pointed out to them that "they" (you know that "unnamed group of experts") said all technological advances from the time of Genesis to 1980 were duplicated in the ten years from 1980 to 1990. Then, all technology from the time of Genesis to 1990 was duplicated in the five years from 1990 to 1995. I went on to point out that according to the *Law of Acceleration*, as it is known, by the year 2000, if we continued doing the same thing for more than six months, it would be passé. Well, here we sit more than a decade later, and we realize that whatever we are doing today is probably old already. So change and flexibility are the order of the day.

I mention this to stress the accuracy of Adizes's assertion that to be a true leader you must demonstrate personally, and practice professionally, *the ability to be flexible and change.*

On Leading

Some organizations have famously manifested inflexibility...to their peril. A classic example is how, in the early 1990s, International Business Machine (IBM) experienced one of the biggest falls from grace in business history. Having been the innovator and role model in the 1980s for many organizations, IBM simply became very content with its position in the *business machine* marketplace and closed its *corporate mind* to the idea that computers would become popular for personal use. IBM suddenly found itself overtaken by Compac, a relatively unknown competitor.

There are other stunning examples of this *contentment* syndrome. Marks and Spencer, the clothier known famously for being the first British retailer to make a pretax profit of over £1 billion in 1998, for example, has been battling for many years to maintain its customer base *due to inflexibility about the way it has been managed.*

Do you remember when the Swiss decided that making digital watches was not for them? They said the Japanese could have that market because that was not true *watch making* and the fad would not last. Now they are making digital watches. I wonder how many billions of dollars this twenty-plus-year hiatus cost the Swiss? If only they had not been adverse to change.

Look at the American auto industry as an example. I know I don't have to spell out for any reader what has happened here. If, thirty years ago, the American auto industry would have been prepared to change their manufacturing mind-set toward smaller, more fuel-efficient cars, the Japanese automakers would never have gotten the foothold in the American marketplace that they now dominate.

Being able to change and adapt is essential. This means you need to be open-minded and flexible, but remember, **when introducing change**

to individuals in your company, doing it in "bite-sized pieces," in which your team can experience success, is vital. These small steps start to mount up, to create a critical mass of positive experiences and, hence, confidence in the new system.

I have learned that when leaders implement change they need to define their objectives. Leaders must set an inspiring goal. You can't aim without a target. Values and Visions are what touch people's souls, unleashing tremendous energy.

Successful businesses are invariably *learning businesses*, which by definition means that business will change its *modus operandi* as it learns. You have to keep up, stay informed, and stay relevant if you want to be a good leader. Being a good leader requires attention, effort, self-awareness, and feedback, none of which just happens of its own accord.

> Let us just look for a moment at this cautionary tale. America had at one point two giants in the business machine industry. There was again International Business Machine (IBM) and also National Cash Register (NCR). Two relatively parallel companies. Enormous! Established! Successful! Going downhill! Well, change was the order of the day for both companies if they wanted to regain their former status in the business place. After its epic fall, IBM made a dramatic change. They hired a CEO, Lou Gerstner, who had no experience in the computer industry. In fact, he came from the tobacco industry. This was a dramatic change because the new CEO had new ideas and much was changed in the company. Mr. Gerstner's view on turning around a company was based on his quote, "I think that my leadership style is to get people to fear staying in one place, to fear not changing." Then we have NCR—who basically decided

to continue to do what they had always done, and have their company run by lawyers and accountants. They only tried to clean up their act a bit. Well, look what happened. IBM learned from their mistake, exercised flexibility, embraced change, and regained their top position. NCR is no longer a factor in the marketplace in which they were once a leader.

> "When you are green you are growing,
> When you are ripe you are rotting."
> *Ray Kroc*
> *Established the McDonald's brand*

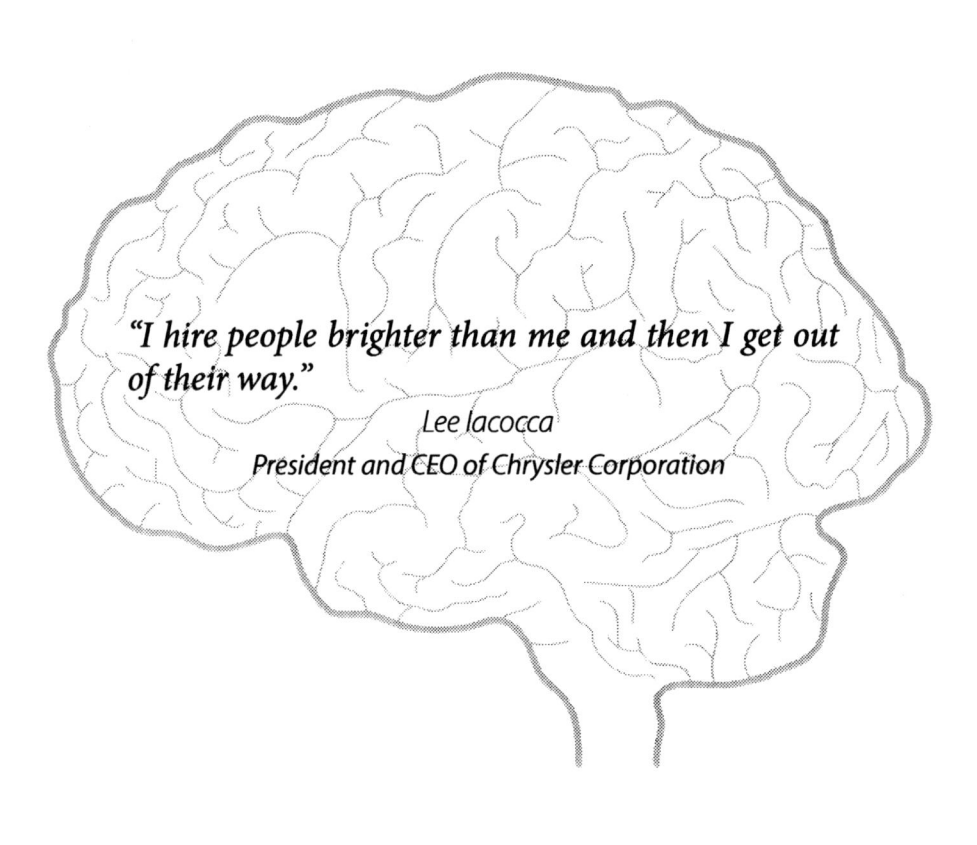

"I hire people brighter than me and then I get out of their way."

Lee Iacocca
President and CEO of Chrysler Corporation

COMMON SENSE MATTERS

On Leading

Hiring Smart... *Surround yourself with people who can "do it better" than you!*

Hiring the right people is possibly the most crucial facet of having a successful business.

- First-rate players hire first-rate players. Second-rate players hire third-rate players.
- Weak leaders are too scared to hire "A" players. "They may outshine me..."
- Bottom line: You cannot have an "A" organization with "B" personnel.

TALENT
Talent is the greatest attribute you can have in an employee. And talent is hard to find. So, <u>*if you find a talented person, hire them even if you don't need them at that moment*</u>. If they are a true talent, they will make themselves productive, and in the long term you will be grateful for your foresight. And if you find this person, pay them well. *Robert Bosch, the great industrialist and inventor of the spark plug, said, "I don't pay good wages because I have a lot of money. I have a lot of money because I pay good wages."*

Rick Goings, who stepped in as Tupperware Brands president in 1992, had a challenge in taking over a company that was hemorrhaging money. He changed the focus of Tupperware to an area he felt was most important. He took his focus off of strategies, tactics, finance, etc., and moved it on to cultivating productive, talented people. He maintained that a company is ultimately a collection of people. He said that if you hired the right people, empowered them, developed them—THAT is how you would get the greatest results in any company. His philosophy paid handsome dividends and the performance of Tupperware was turned around.

OK, so let's talk about the <u>process</u> for finding the right *human* resources for your business.

Step # 1. Identify six to ten <u>behavioral traits</u> of your top *successful* employees in a specific position. You will need different behavioral traits for, say, a salesperson as compared to a comptroller, e.g., if you are looking for a comptroller, the traits you may be looking for could include attention to detail, discernment, sensitivity to meeting deadlines, etc. Whereas, if you are hiring a salesperson, the traits could include healthy but not obnoxious ego, drive, service orientation, will to win, etc. This is because you must **not** hire the <u>person</u>. You **must** hire the <u>behavior</u> they bring to the workplace for that specific position—self-confidence, discernment, ego, energy, sociability, tact, attention to detail, etc., etc. These become your <u>benchmarks</u>.

Step #2. Create five to ten questions in each category (examples above) that will typify this specific behavior. Structure each question in such a way that the answer can be rated by the interviewer on a scale of one to ten.

Step #3. Have your top two or three current employees in each job category answer the questionnaire. You can even go outside your company to people who are stars in your industry. Their ego, if you know them, will usually persuade them to answer these questions for you. When this is done, you will have a graph of the behavioral traits of the most talented people currently in each position. You now create a graph that is the average of these top performers in each category, and this will become your benchmark for this position. (See example below).

Step # 4. When interviewing each applicant, have the interviewer complete the interview questionnaire for the benchmarked behaviors of that position. I like to suggest that this part of the interview process is done by phone when setting up the interview appointment. The reasons for this are (1) You can see if there is no chance of a match for the position. Then you will not waste your time doing an hour-long interview; and (2) You will not be influenced by the "appearance" of the applicant. You will be looking only at the behavioral traits, which is what you are hiring.

You can now create a graph of their answers related to <u>their behaviors</u> **and then superimpose it over the graph of the average of your best performers for that position**. The two or three candidates whose graphs fit closest to your benchmarks should be the <u>only</u> people interviewed and considered for the job. Be objective and disciplined. It is because so many hiring decisions are made on what the person looks like, or speaks like, instead of what the person's <u>behaviors</u> are, that the majority of companies have large turnover—or have C+ performers. Which Human Resources (HR) Department doesn't want to hire Brad Pitt or Angelina Jolie, instead of someone more "homely," even if their behavior doesn't fit the requirements of the position, contributing to high turnover?

THE BEHAVIORAL TRAITS OF A PERSON DEFINE THEIR TALENT FOR THAT POSITION.

See below what your graph may look like. If the applicant's scores do not closely match the benchmarked scores, then ***it does not matter how much you like the applicant—do not employ them.***

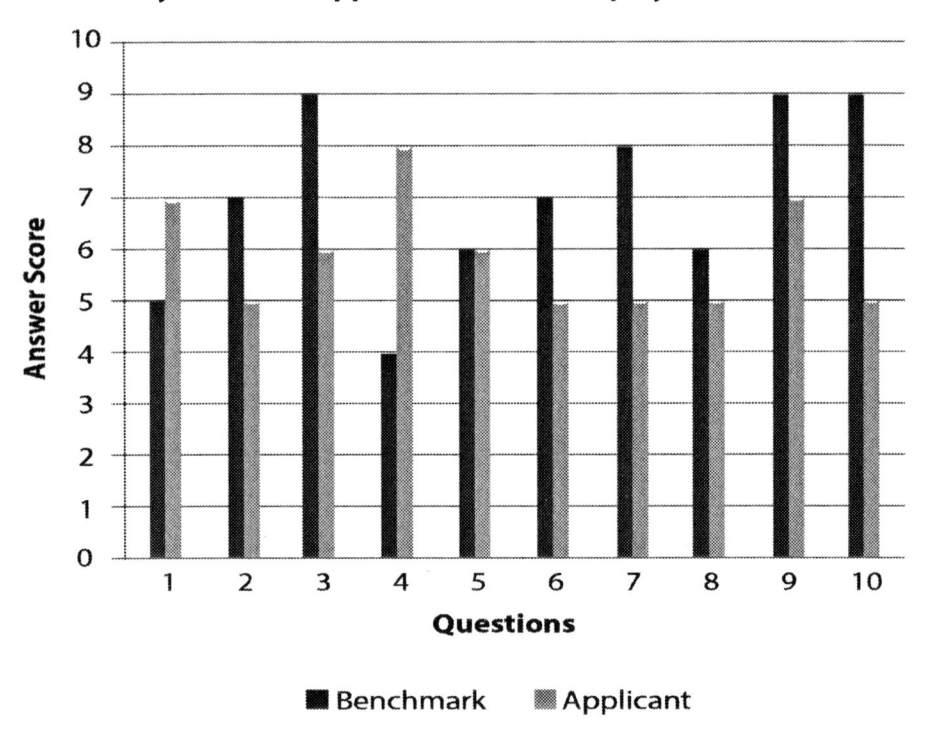

```
Benchmark vs Applicant scores by Question:
Q1: Benchmark 5, Applicant 7
Q2: Benchmark 7, Applicant 5
Q3: Benchmark 9, Applicant 6
Q4: Benchmark 4, Applicant 8
Q5: Benchmark 6, Applicant 6
Q6: Benchmark 7, Applicant 5
Q7: Benchmark 8, Applicant 5
Q8: Benchmark 6, Applicant 5
Q9: Benchmark 9, Applicant 7
Q10: Benchmark 9, Applicant 5
```

This graph based on the questions you designed measures the TALENT you are looking for—not the EXPERIENCE.

My suggestion is that an applicant should be within 10 percent of the benchmark on 80 percent of the questions. But understand that each industry is different, and you must select the norm for your industry.

*An employee brings three things to the table: Talent (**T**), Experience (**E**), Chemistry (**C**).*
*It would be best to hire someone who brings all three, **T, E,** and **C**. This rarely happens.*
*The next best choice is to bring someone in that brings **T** and **C** to the table.*
*The third choice is someone that brings **T** and **E** to the table.*

You see, you cannot teach Talent or good Chemistry, **but you can give Experience**.

If you follow this rule, in a year you will have a **"T E C"** ("A" player) on your staff. It should be noted, however, that the **T** player is a *must*. If the person is an above average **C**, then the final result you will have is a B+ team member (not all that shabby). If you don't hire the **T** or the **C**, you will <u>NEVER</u> have an "A" player in that position.

An **A** player has **T, E,** and **C**.
If a **B** player has **T** and **C**, they can get **E** and become an **A**.
If a **B** player has **T** and **E**, they cannot get **C** and can never become an **A**.

Ensure that 80 percent of your employees are **A**s and **B**s, <u>and never ever hire lower than that grade</u>.

I have used the above process for many years, with great success. I want to share with you two stories about two people I hired, where this process enabled me to identify that they would be winners.

> *First was a gentleman named Jan. He applied for a job with me as a salesperson. Previously, he was fired as bus driver from the*

Johannesburg Tramways. He went on to tell me that he stopped his bus to get a quick cup of coffee, as he was ahead of schedule, when some prankster stepped into the bus, which was full of passengers, and drove it twenty miles out of town. He felt the firing was unwarranted, as he was ahead of schedule. Hmmmm!

This man sat across the desk from me, in a frayed shirt, with dirt on his shoes and broken fingernails, telling me he wanted to be a salesman. When I asked him why he wanted to sell, his response was, "I was fired from the tramways department. The only thing lower than that is selling." Well, there was just something about Jan that made me give him the test I describe above. His profile blew me out of the water. The end result (two years later) was that he ended up my top Regional Sales Manager. When he followed me to live in America, he sold his Mercedes and his mortgage-free house. I mustn't forget to mention that he now dressed like he had just stepped out of GQ. The process worked. The behavior—not the appearance—identified his talent.

The next story of a superstar whom I identified by this process was a man called Wies. He applied for a job as an Operations/Project Manager. Halfway through the interview, he interrupted me and said (and I am paraphrasing here), "Sir, I think we are getting on well together, so before we go any further, I feel I must confess to you that I have just gotten out of jail. I murdered a man. I choked him to death—but I had good reason. After serving eight years of my sentence, I was released with the recent amnesty granted by the president to fifty prisoners." I liked Wies's honesty and started to ask him the questions that would show me if he had a talent worth pursuing. The answers he gave me encouraged me to give him the behavioral test.

Well, he hit the ball out of the park. The process I am sharing with you worked again. If I had to rate all my successful hires, he would certainly be in the top three.

TIME TO "LET GO"
Let me say here there are many clichés about hiring slow and firing fast. Well, if you hire right, you may not have to fire that often, but obviously, from time to time, firing is a must. And let me say I don't prescribe to the principle of firing the bottom 5 percent of your employees every year (irrespective of how good they are) to keep everyone else on their toes, as some companies prescribe.

I want to share a principle with you that has worked very well for me in my businesses. When you start thinking about letting someone go, it is already time to pull the trigger. Don't meditate on the decision. Make the decision. Once you have determined that experience and coaching have not elevated the employee to the necessary level, don't think on how you can "save" them. That is not the business you are in—"saving people." If you don't let that person go when you first realize it is necessary, you will spend untold hours pondering a decision that will be inevitable anyway, at some point. That time could be better spent focusing on the positive aspects of your business that will make money and move you toward your goals.

> *Caution:*
> *When hiring someone who indicates to you that their experience level is ten years—please make sure they don't mean one year's experience, ten times.*

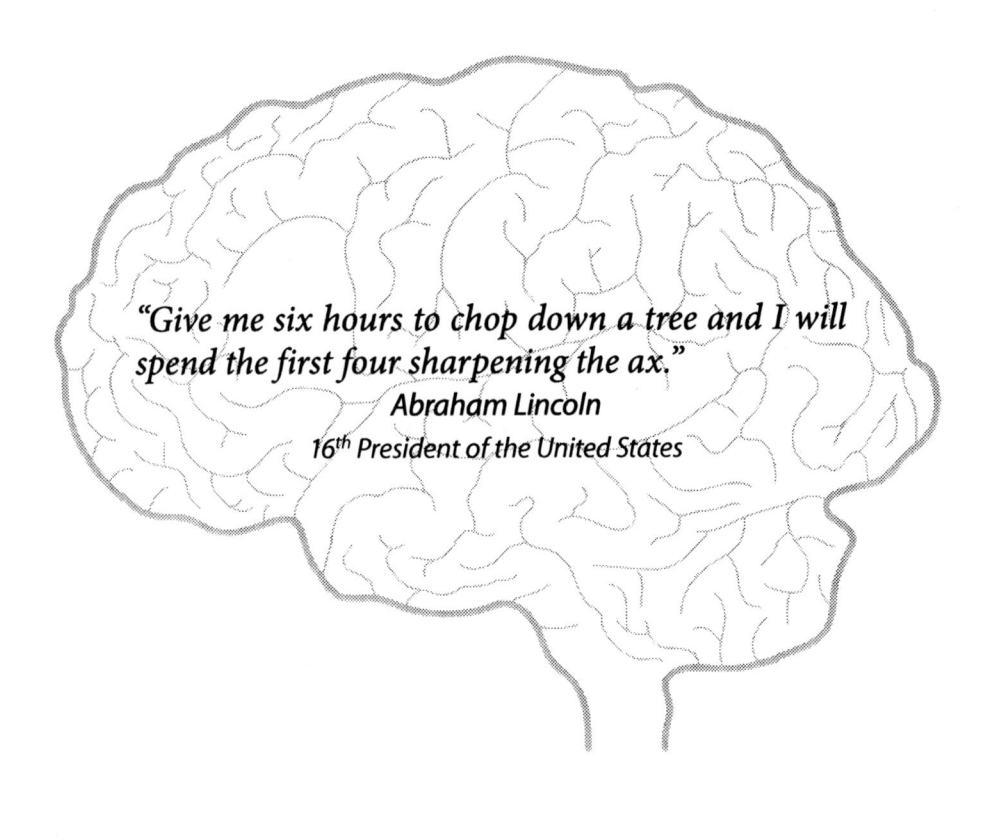

"Give me six hours to chop down a tree and I will spend the first four sharpening the ax."
Abraham Lincoln
16th President of the United States

COMMON SENSE MATTERS

On Leading

A Roadmap to Success...*Plan from the top down—and work from the bottom up*
Spend less time working in your business and more time working <u>on</u> your business.

The roadmap I am talking about here is your business plan—not the one you use for raising capital and then never read again. There are two types of business plans. One is used for raising money. If you own your business and you are looking for investors or a bank loan, your business plan will be more conventional than the one we will examine in this chapter. The plan here is a real, live, working plan, to which all the participants in the business refer on a regular basis. It is also a plan that can be used by departmental or divisional heads for their areas of management.

I created this model because I saw too many companies develop business plans for lending institutions or banks, and once the transaction was complete, never look at that plan again to run the business. This hit me hardest when I was party to a newly formed company that was looking for an underwriter to raise over $70 million for a public offering. Once the underwriters were on board and the company was an ongoing concern, the business plan was never looked at again. What a shame!! The business never got off the ground, notwithstanding the plan was a good one *because management did not perform according to the written business plan.*

This is what my "Business Plan Blueprint" looks like:

Vision: Where would you like your company to be in three to five years? The world is changing so fast now, to plan for any time longer than this would be unreasonable.

Mission: An <u>annual</u> statement, defining where you would like your company to be at the end of that specific year. This changes from year to year because the business environment is constantly changing. Many people find it difficult to create a mission statement. A great way to start is to ask the top four or five people that you work with to give you *one word* they think best describes your company, e.g., service, profit, respect, dedication, growth. Then create *one sentence* using most or all of these words, and you will have your mission statement. However, please, when developing a mission statement, don't let it be a generic statement that would fit any company, in any industry. This is an opportunity for you to separate yourself from the crowd. Be unique. Be different. Make your statement memorable.

Goals: What you want to achieve in different divisions within your business, e.g., you can have a sales goal, a profit goal, a growth goal, a product line goal, etc., etc.—but it is imperative that all goals are <u>measurable</u>. The BIG SECRET to making this process successful is that <u>all your goals, added together, must equal your mission.</u>

Objective: A subsection of each goal, e.g., if a goal is to show a higher profit, one of the objectives could be to attract more sales (be specific). Another objective for the same goal could be to cut expenses (once again, be specific on the total dollar amount). Once again, <u>all your objectives, added together, must equal the goal to which they apply.</u> Then you will develop Strategies in order to achieve each objective.

Strategies: This is the plan of action to achieve your objectives. The strategies to attracting more sales could be: new product lines, new territories, better sales coaching, or an upgraded sales force (hiring "A" salespeople instead of "B" s). <u>Once again, all your strategies added together should achieve the objective.</u>

Action Items: The specific steps to fulfill your strategies, and with them, the same principal applies, e.g., if you wanted to add new product lines, you would need to do market research, determine product costs, determine marketing costs, etc. And <u>all your action items added together must equal the strategy to which they apply.</u>

This is what the plan looks like:

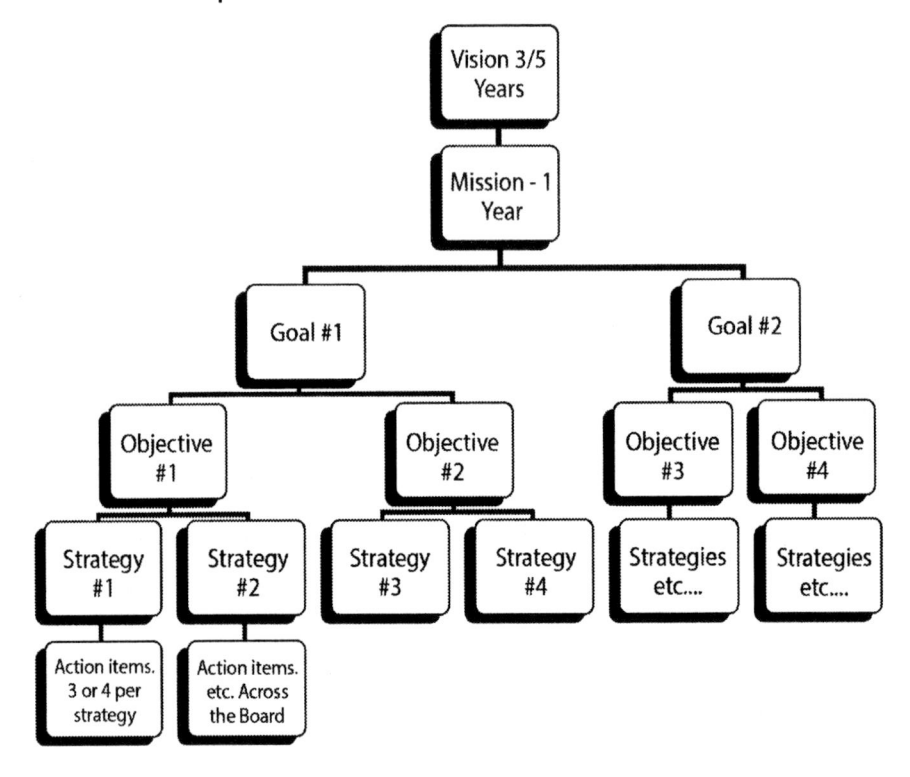

```
                    ┌──────────────┐
                    │  Vision 3/5  │
                    │    Years     │
                    └──────┬───────┘
                           │
                    ┌──────┴───────┐
                    │  Mission - 1 │
                    │     Year     │
                    └──────┬───────┘
              ┌────────────┴────────────┐
         ┌────┴────┐                ┌────┴────┐
         │ Goal #1 │                │ Goal #2 │
         └────┬────┘                └────┬────┘
        ┌────┴────┐                ┌────┴────┐
   ┌────┴───┐ ┌───┴────┐      ┌────┴───┐ ┌───┴────┐
   │Objective│ │Objective│     │Objective│ │Objective│
   │   #1   │ │   #2   │      │   #3   │ │   #4   │
   └───┬────┘ └───┬────┘      └───┬────┘ └───┬────┘
    ┌──┴──┐   ┌──┴──┐          ┌──┴──┐     │
 ┌──┴─┐┌──┴─┐┌┴───┐┌┴───┐   ┌──┴──┐ ┌──┴──┐
 │Stra││Stra││Stra││Stra│   │Strat│ │Strat│
 │tegy││tegy││tegy││tegy│   │egies│ │egies│
 │ #1 ││ #2 ││ #3 ││ #4 │   │etc..│ │etc..│
 └─┬──┘└─┬──┘└────┘└────┘   └─────┘ └─────┘
 ┌─┴──┐┌─┴────┐
 │Action││Action│
 │items.││items.│
 │3 or 4││etc. Across│
 │per   ││the Board│
 │strategy││     │
 └──────┘└──────┘
```

- ➢ <u>VISION</u>- CEO, to be managed by owner, in conjunction with his leadership team
- ➢ <u>MISSION/GOALS</u>- CEO, to be managed by owner, and/or VPs, in conjunction with their leadership team (one level down)
- ➢ <u>OBJECTIVES</u> and Strategies- to be managed by upper management
- ➢ <u>ACTION ITEMS</u>- to be managed by supervisors, team leaders

NOW the <u>planning</u> process is over. You planned from the TOP DOWN, and the plan gets <u>implemented</u> by working it from the BOTTOM UP.

This is how it works:

- Do not have more than four goals, because then the plan will become too cumbersome.
- In some smaller businesses/models, it may not be necessary to have all the steps.
- The person responsible for any goal, objective, strategy, or action item must understand that if any segment is not completed properly, the entire equation will not work.

When I came to live in the United States (1981), I needed to build a strong medium-sized company that had a national presence, in a five-year time frame. I used the plan shown above, and it made delegation and the management process relatively simple for me. But more importantly, it gave me a tool to measure and manage the process and the results I was looking to achieve. In the delegation layout, a VP was responsible for each goal. That was his/her focus. They then appointed specific people to handle each objective in each field of responsibility. This meant they had three or four people reporting to them who each had an objective to achieve. The same process then applied to the strategies and action Items.

The process was a resounding success. In our fourth year in business, we did over fifty-five million dollars in sales and had branch offices in thirteen states.

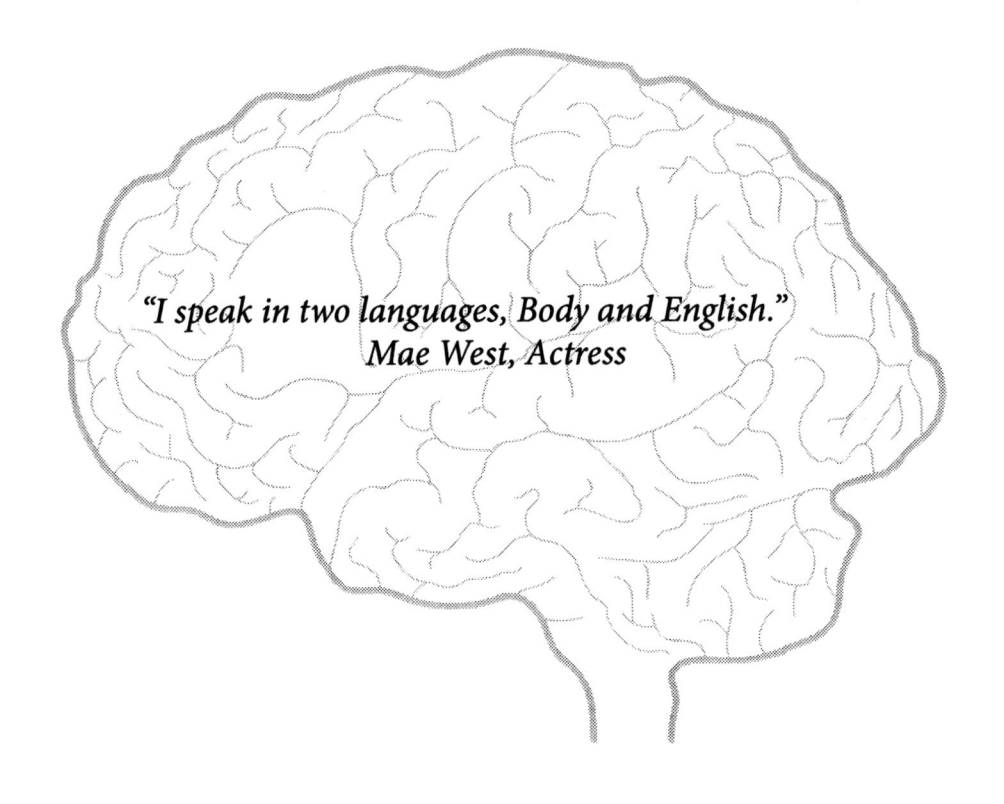

"I speak in two languages, Body and English."
Mae West, Actress

COMMON SENSE MATTERS

On Leading

Communicate*...Speak in conversation, not monologue*

At the outset, let us understand that only 7 percent of communication is verbal; the other 93 percent is nonverbal intonations, attitude, tone, body language, volume, etc. This is why two people can use the same words and convey a completely different message.

One can never overestimate the importance of good, no, *great* communicating skills. And in a leadership role, the ability to communicate well is even more critical.

The top three critical facets to good communication are:

1. The ability to <u>listen</u>.
2. The ability to <u>interpret</u>, and use, body language effectively.
3. The ability to <u>make others understand</u> what you are trying to communicate.

When providing leadership, be it for a company or a project, it is not sufficient to circulate global e-mails or post notices around the offices or plant. There must be a significant amount of *face-to-face* communication. People at the front line need to feel involved and know that their opinions are taken into account about how new structures, processes, and procedures are implemented. In almost every organization, people complain that there is not "enough communication." The reality, however, is often quite the opposite—too much communication takes place. Everyone is deluged with e-mails, texts, and memos. We often seem to be drowning in information overload. What is needed is *effective communication*, which involves face-to-face contact sessions, dialogue, and the opportunity for people to meet and discuss key issues. As our ability to communicate grows, we must not lose sight of the fact that human beings are emotional animals. We must not allow human contact, briefing sessions, management by walking around, and focus groups to be replaced by global e-mails, video conferencing, and electronic messaging. People need the stimulation of human communication, particularly in times of challenge and uncertainty.

When we came into this life, we were given two ears and one mouth—and they should be used in that proportion. At all times, we need to listen *at least twice as much as we speak*. And there is an art to orchestrating this well. If you know (or learn) how to ask the right questions, you will be amazed at the details you get in your answers. Most people love to respond to questions because it shows you value their opinions. (A good point to remember is that the quality of your answers is directly related to the quality of your questions.). At that point, you **shut up and listen,** interjecting the occasional "I see" or "I understand" or "can you elaborate on that please," which shows you are absorbing what is being said.

When communicating with others in writing, two points are really important. Firstly, be clear, short, to the point, and succinct. And secondly, do it regularly. Always follow up your communications, whether it is in writing or verbal. The exception to this is social media-type communications, where the information is intended to reach many people.

Wherever possible, in e-mails or inter-office memoranda, it is proven that short bullet points get the best response. The content is clear and understandable, and the paragraphs don't have to be read and reread.

The interpretation of gestures as nonverbal communication is *kinesics*, and there is an entire field of study dedicated to it. We know it better as *body language*—and there are a few basic common sense rules that can help you benefit from it.

Probably the most important thing to know is that you can build rapport with the person you are talking to if **you mirror <u>their</u> body language**. If they are relaxed, you relax. If they are leaning forward in their chair, you lean forward in your chair. If they are sitting, you sit. If they are animated, you get animated. As they change their positions, you change your positions. The only things you do not mimic are folded arms and crossed legs. In fact, if you are communicating with someone whose arms are folded, it probably means their mind is also closed—so get them to unfold their arms. This can normally be done by handing them something to look at or to read.

We all know and understand that eye contact is extremely important. The eyes are the windows to the soul. When you look at someone's eyes, try to see if they are engrossed in what you are saying. If not, ask them a nonchallenging question and see whether their eyes soften. They normally will. Just be wary when following the rule of looking into someone's eyes when you are talking to them. There are two possible pitfalls. One is that you may be too intense, and it may be a bit intimidating. And secondly, which eye do you look at, the left one or the right one? I usually find that looking at the bridge of the person's nose, with glances going from one eye to the other, is the most comfortable (for both of you).

Trade terms are great if you are communicating with someone in your trade. If not, be wary of them. They can come back and bite you in the "you know where."

A good example is when trade terms are used by the communicator and are not understood by the listener. The listener does not want to be embarrassed by their ignorance, so they do not ask for clarification, but they then mentally change stations and tune out of the conversation.

> *When I was nineteen, I wanted to buy an insurance policy that would force me to save money that I would then be able to cash in at some later stage in my life. Well, the agent kept talking to me about an "annuity." I didn't know what an annuity was. I was too embarrassed to ask. I didn't buy. He didn't sell. We both lost.*

For your communication to be clearly understood, these elements must all be in sync:

- **Verbal—*Be careful of the words you use***
- **Vocal—*Be cautious of the tone in which you say them***
- **Visual—*Be conscious of your body language and theirs***

Speak WITH your Team,
Not AT them!

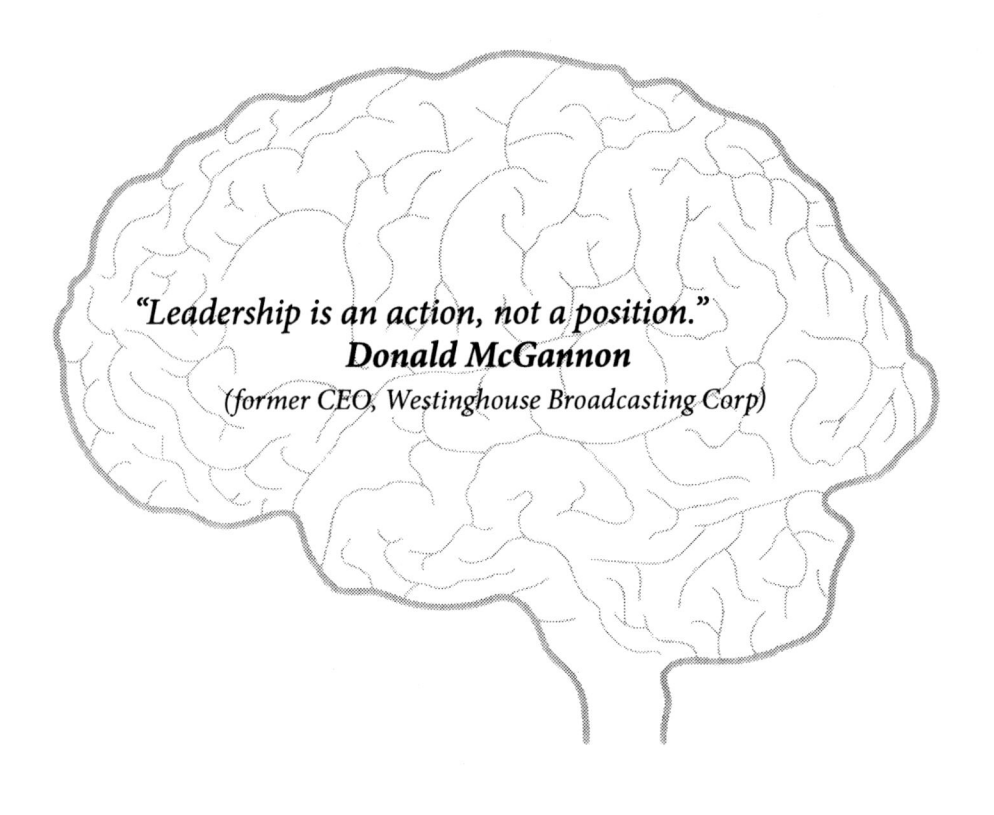

"Leadership is an action, not a position."
Donald McGannon
(former CEO, Westinghouse Broadcasting Corp)

COMMON SENSE MATTERS

On Leading

Be Open with Employees... They want authenticity, not perfection, in their leader

Leaders must be transparent with their employees. This is especially true when it comes to opening up about your own pros and cons. Yet not enough leaders do it. One third of American employees say their bosses are not open enough about their strengths and weaknesses, or that of their company, as they should be.

Embrace transparency. When leaders come to terms with and grasp their own positives and negatives, it tends to open things up so the team no longer feels the need to be flawless. What people want in a leader is not perfection, it is authenticity. When candidates run for the highest office in the land, they all preach "transparency" over and over again. Then, if they get elected, invariably that promise goes down the tubes. On a continuing basis we read about and hear of things the administration is doing that no one knew about. And so seeds of discontent and distrust are sown. We learn that whether it is a government or a business with only a few employees, having your people plugged into the truth will always build confidence and respect for the leader.

Be open. Communication with employees is essential. Unless your employees know you and know about you, you will not be able to take the company in the direction you want it to go.

On Leading

In one position I held, where I had eighty-five direct and indirect reports, their previous manager had been let go. One of his major failings was that he could not get on with his staff, mainly because he did not communicate well with them and was never open with them. Upon taking the position, I had a psychological test done on myself. It showed my strengths and weaknesses, my likes and dislikes. In fact, it mentally undressed me. When I got this report, I made eighty-five copies and gave them to everyone who reported (down the line) to me. They now <u>knew</u> me! Even seemingly insignificant things about me. My staff knew I didn't like long phone calls…get to the point…don't lie to me…I am a stickler for the truth, no matter how bad it may seem…reports need to be in bullet-point form…always be on time for appointments…etc., etc., etc.

My relationship with the staff was great, and tremendous relationships were built in conjunction with friendships—which, in turn, delivered great business results.

> *Honesty is such a lonely word*
> *Everyone is so untrue.*
> *Honesty is hardly ever heard*
> *And mostly what I need from you.*
>   *"Honesty"*
>   *Billy Joel*

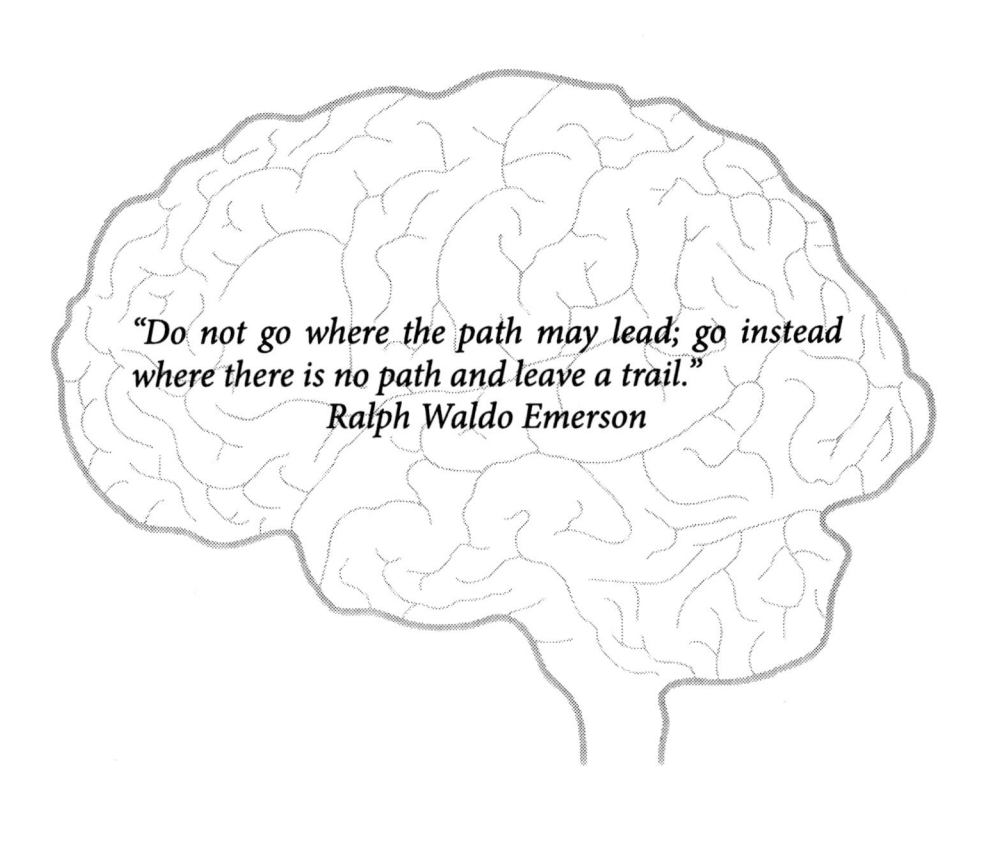

> *"Do not go where the path may lead; go instead where there is no path and leave a trail."*
> *Ralph Waldo Emerson*

COMMON SENSE MATTERS

On Leading

Take Time to Think…Ready, AIM, Fire always works best!

How you think is everything. Always be positive. Think success, not failure. Beware of a negative environment.

When you go to the gym, you exercise. The more you exercise, the stronger your muscles get. Well, your brain is no different. The more it exercises, the stronger it gets. When you are fit, you <u>want</u> to exercise—and you exercise well; the same principle applies to your brain. It needs and wants exercise. The more it exercises, the better it will function. And the exercise for your brain is thinking. Reading, planning, doing Sudoku, working crosswords, visualizing, etc. is all exercise for the brain—and it thrives on exercise. Ask any doctor and they will tell you doing things like crosswords are some of the best exercises to delay the onset of Alzheimer's disease.

Some of the most productive times I have ever had were when I took a door hanger and hung it on the outside handle of my office door. It simply said:

"DO NOT DISTURB—as I am being productive right now."

This was when I focused on an idea or tried to solve a problem without people interrupting my thought process by asking me questions or wanting to share a tidbit. My phone would be-turned off, I would have no outside influences interrupting me, and I could be completely centered.

Let me give you an example: Say I am looking to sell a specific service or product (either for myself or on behalf of a client; for instance, a heat pump for a swimming pool). After I have closed my door, I get behind my desk—sometimes put my feet up—close my eyes and transport myself to a swimming pool in the fall. I am sitting poolside; I can smell the outdoors, a poolside cocktail, or even maybe the sun block. I walk to the pool edge and start down the steps into the water. The temperature shocks me. I can't envisage swimming in water that cool. I then start to think what could be said to me at that point that would get me to buy a heat pump that would make the water comfortable. I then envisage the same procedure getting into warm water at a pre-selected temperature. I feel the joy. I feel the benefits. Then with these thoughts in mind, I can develop an empathetic marketing program or sales presentation for that product. Done in less than thirty minutes, and then my door is opened again.

I often find the best way to think is to think backward. I think of the outcome first, then I think of what the steps "prior" to the outcome are. When I have that, I take one step back again and continue doing this until I am at genesis. Suddenly the plan is automatically "there."

Remember: it's not "Ready, FIRE, Aim"…

Take time to THINK

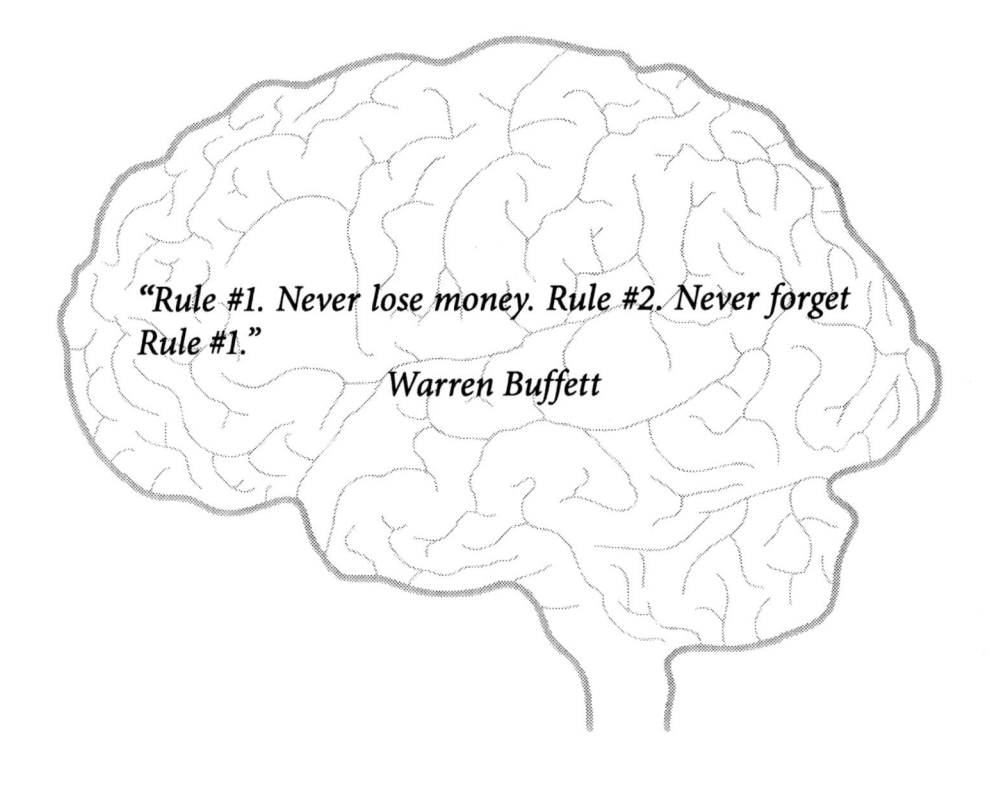

"Rule #1. Never lose money. Rule #2. Never forget Rule #1."
  Warren Buffett

COMMON SENSE MATTERS

On Leading

***Trim the Fat**...Always run your business as if times are tough*

Let us reflect back to the recession of 2008 for a moment.

We had businesses coming off the seven years of plenty suddenly being hit with bad economic news. The housing market collapse. The stock market in the doldrums. Factory orders disappearing into thin air. Panic started to set in at most boardrooms across the country. The "boardroom" may have been in a big, publically held company or a husband and wife team sitting in their living room. Most companies and/or people felt the squeeze coming and everyone was planning on the best way to handle it for their situation.

- **Some companies decided to do whatever it took to get more sales.**
    - *Invariably, their margins were cut because they were buying business.*
- **Some companies decided to cut expenses by reducing staff or cutting salaries.**
    - *When this happens, people start to fear for their job, internal politics take hold, and motivation among the staff becomes a challenge.*

- **_Some companies cut certain general & administrative expenses._**
  - _This can put undue burden on the already reduced staff, and services to customers and employees may suffer._

While these are all good strategies, they come with a price. What is the best solution? Chase more sales. But in a recession this is very difficult because you must watch your gross margin dollars more than you watch your <u>sales numbers</u>. You may _need_ to reduce your staff and/or cut salaries if you want to be in business for the long term—and this brings with it psychological challenges for the employees and the leaders.

So, the REAL solution is to run your company efficiently in the good times—so you will not have to do anything drastic in the bad times. CUT THE FAT WHEN TIMES ARE GOOD, then you won't have to when times get tough—because you will have a war chest. I know this is easier said than done, but strong leaders must have vision, and this principle will test their mettle. And as we all know, everything in life is cyclical, so bad times will follow good times—and good times will follow bad. The only variable is the timing.

When times are good, run your business as if times are tough. I guarantee that when you cut 10 percent of your workforce intelligently, the other 90 percent step up their efforts so you don't lose any productivity.

> _You may agree with the philosophy of one of the most successful CEOs of all time, Jack Welsh of General Electric fame. Often thought of as the best CEO in America, he had a philosophy of letting <u>the bottom 5 percent of his staff go every year</u>, irrespective of how good they were. According to Welch in an Esquire_

Magazine article "What I've Learned," (December 31, 2006, by Cal Fussman) the worst kind of manager is one who practices "false kindness." Says Welch, "You think you're a nice manager—that you're a kind manager? Well guess what? You won't be there someday. You'll be promoted. Or you'll retire. And a new manager will come in and look at the employee and say 'Hey, you're not that good.' And all of a sudden this employee is now fifty-three, fifty-five, with fewer options in life. And now you're gonna tell him 'go home'? How is that kind? You are the cruelest kind of manager." <u>Welch always maintained that nobody was ever surprised when they were let go.</u>

I must confess, I believe he is 90 percent correct with this assertion.

The bottom line: When times are good, run your business as if you are entering a recession. Another option is to always have your corporate structure and your financials looking *good enough to sell* your business—even if you are not looking to put it on the market. Monitor even the smallest expense and fight for every point in gross margin. Then when the next recession comes—and I guarantee it will—the changes you will need to make in your business will be minimal.

Plan for the worst and hope for the best.

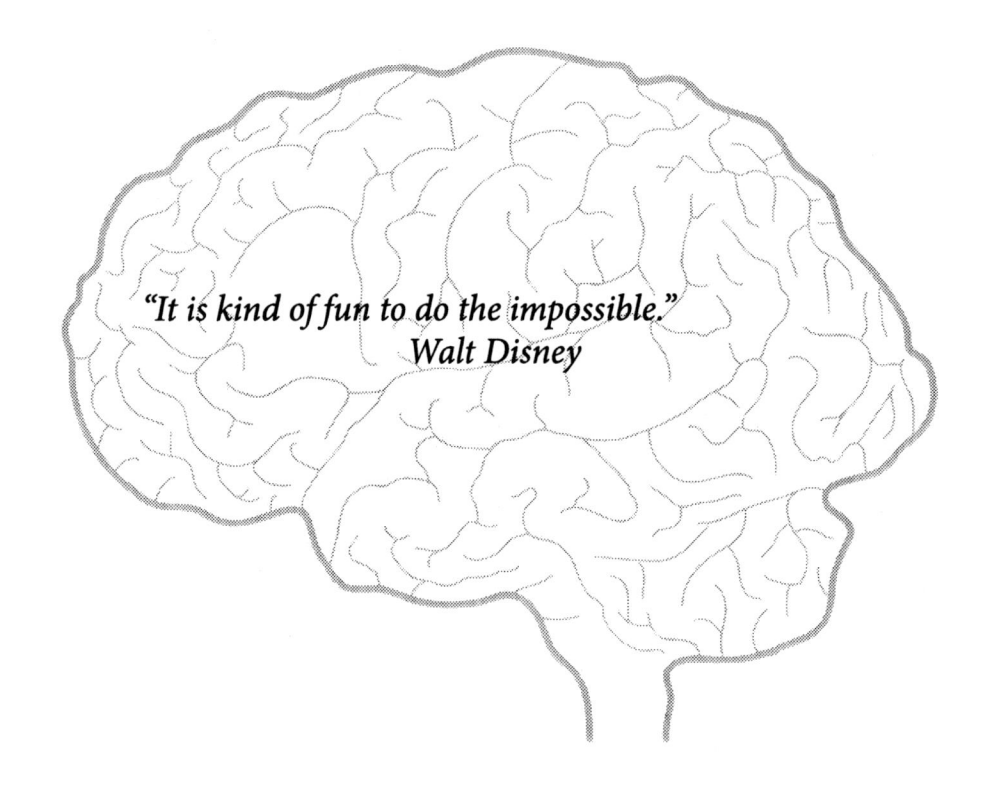

"It is kind of fun to do the impossible."
Walt Disney

COMMON SENSE MATTERS

On Leading

Incentivize and Motivate... *Use honey, not a big stick.*

An observation I have always found valid is that you can tell a motivated organization by the spring in the employees' steps and the glint in their eyes. This is *lasting* motivation. Giving someone a prize of some sort, so they feel great at that moment, is short-term motivation. It will only last until they go downstairs and find someone has put a ding in their car, or they use the check you just gave them to take their significant other out to dinner. Then all their short-term motivation is a thing of the past.

Real motivation is a climate, an ambience, a culture. It permeates an organization. When you can feel it, sense it, and taste it—then it is everlasting.

I believe most leaders know motivation can take two forms: reward and recognition. But it is my contention that the most important part of motivation is that a company should have a climate of motivation, an *ambience* of motivation permeating throughout the entire organization. In the hallways. In the offices. In the passages. At the water cooler. In communicating. In body language. You get the message, I am sure.

On Leading

To have a motivated organization, you must create this climate and culture. THE MORALE OF A COMPANY IS NOT BUILT FROM THE BOTTOM UP—IT FILTERS FROM THE TOP DOWN.

This does not mean you should not incentivize staff. You need to do both. A good principle to keep in mind is, **reward *results* and recognize *effort.***

In many instances, an "Atta Boy," or a literal pat on the back, with a few words of thanks, is a tremendous incentive for people to do well.

An e-mail to a project leader, thanking them for their leadership, works wonders. Recognition at team meetings or in-house newsletters and similar actions all help create a *culture of motivation.*

I am also a great proponent of sharing select financial results with the employees. They like to be in the know. They then feel trusted. When they are informed, they tend to take ownership of results. In turn, it helps them understand certain actions you may take in leading the company. This also means that if you have a profit sharing plan for your employees, they can track company progress during the year and know what to expect at the end of the year. Bill Kent, the owner of a leading wholesale distribution company in Florida, does this on a monthly basis, and this philosophy has served his company handsomely since 1969.

> Jack Welch, the ex-CEO of General Electric, said, "Giving people self-confidence is by far the most important thing I can do. Because then they will act."

This is done by sharing successes with the staff. By sharing challenges with the staff. By listening to the staff's problems, suggestions, and comments. By asking the staff for input—in short, by making them feel that they belong. Seek input from your staff. Get feedback, both positive and negative. Be sure they feel it is OK to be honest with you. Otherwise, their comments will not be authentic.

> *You may remember Buddy Ryan, who was the defensive coordinator for the 1985 Chicago Bears (under Mike Ditka). He was great as a defensive coordinator—but after the Bears won the Super Bowl, he was offered a head coaching position with the Philadelphia Eagles. Suddenly, being the head honcho went to his head, and instead of calling his players by their names, he called them by their numbers. "Hey, sixty-seven, come here!" He took being personal and being personable out of his demeanor and leadership style. The consequence was he was a dismal failure as a head coach.*

Let people know you care—because it's the truth.

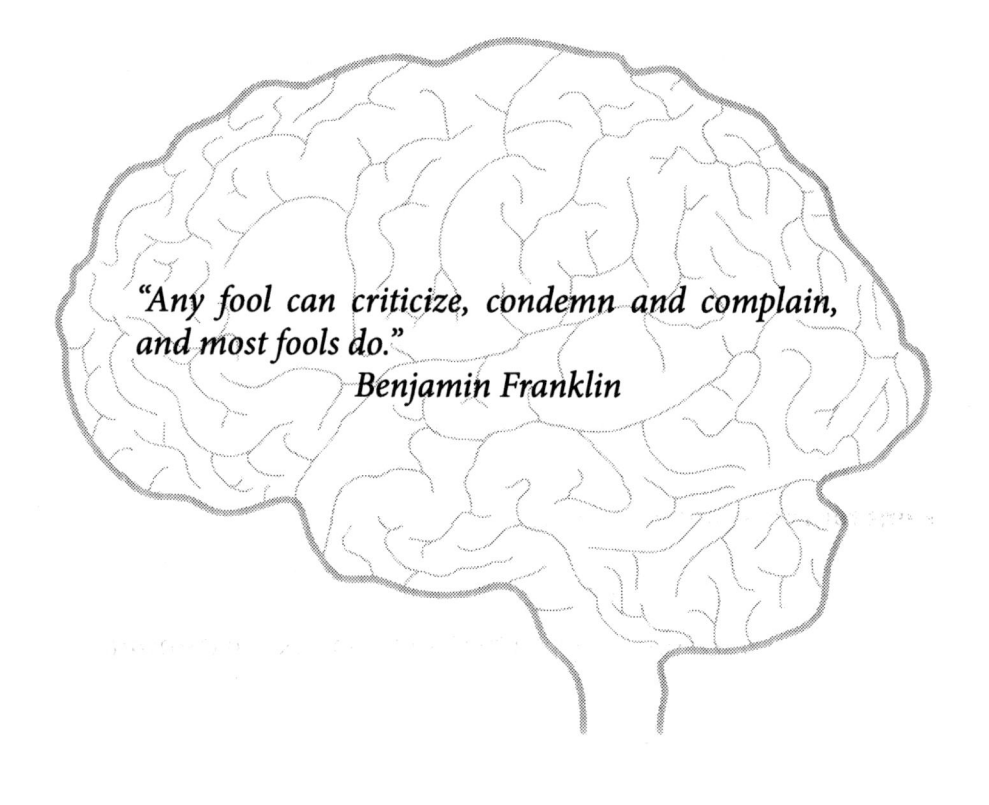

"Any fool can criticize, condemn and complain, and most fools do."
Benjamin Franklin

COMMON SENSE MATTERS

On Leading

Inspire Your Organization... *The worst mistake a boss can make is to not say, "Well done."*

Lift your TEAM: Though the company leader is at the top, leadership is a group effort. Most people look to the leader for vision and the answers to all the problems. Not possible. A true leader calls upon the leadership capabilities of the entire TEAM. This becomes a culture within a company. Now everyone is looking for solutions and planning for the future (of their company, their division, their department, etc.). This is one of the prime ingredients that define a corporate culture.

Hunt for the intangibles. Sure, it's lonely at the top—but minimize that loneliness by surrounding yourself with talented people: people with character, people with the will to win, people with passion, people with courage. Don't only focus on the head, *also focus on the heart*.

Trust. Once you've delegated a task, let the individual or the team get on with the job and do it, without you hovering over their shoulder.

Be Steel and Velvet. Martial arts legend Bruce Lee said the softest substances, like air and water, could penetrate the hardest substances, like rock and granite. Leaders must recognize this phenomenon and realize the necessity for patience and collaboration. And talking about patience, you will read this often from me, "Remember, the positive takes time—only the negative happens quickly."

Think and Plan. As a leader, you should always be planning. When you have planned a project, then plan how you can improve it. Be planning the next step. Be planning five steps ahead. Be planning the best utilization of your resources, people, money, and your own talent. Plan. Plan and then plan again. In today's rapidly changing market, the inimitable advice penned by Benjamin Franklin in the mid-1700s is more valid today than ever. **"By failing to prepare, you are preparing to fail."**

Focus on results. It is too easy to focus on processes and procedures and get bogged down in this quicksand. Leaders need to keep their focus on results. Success is a W in the results column as opposed to an L. Sometimes a W may be ugly, but it is way better than a pretty L.

> *A client of mine engaged my services to help fill the company's CEO position. In addition to the other proven vetting methods I applied, I asked the following question of all the applicants. "What would satisfy you more as the CEO, qualifying for your annual bonus, knowing you only put in 90 percent effort during the year—or missing your bonus but knowing you put in 120 percent effort?"*
>
> *The woman who was ultimately hired was the only person that said the <u>effort you put in is irrelevant</u>—the only thing that counts, <u>as long as you are honest and ethical</u>, is to WIN. She went on to say, "If winning wasn't everything, then why participate? I will surround myself with people who are better than me. I will inspire them, I will motivate them, and with this approach I cannot lose." How many people would watch*

a football game if we didn't keep score? She was, and still is, an unmitigated success. <u>*She has always been solely focused on winning.*</u>

This being said, you must understand this should be the rule for leaders and drivers, not for internal administrative staff. Their objective is not to take actions that make the team win. Their objective is to report back to the CEO and other management staff with FACTS, so they can make the right decision to make the team win. They need to tell decision makers the state of the business, whether the news is good or not. We know that "what gets measured, gets done," and if we are not measuring the true information (in a timely fashion), then good business decisions cannot be made.

*"**Great vision without great people is irrelevant.**"*
Jim Collins, Author, Good to Great

"Number one, cash is king…number two, communicate…number three, buy or bury the competition."
Jack Welch

COMMON SENSE MATTERS

On Leading

It is Not a Sale Until the Cash is in the Bank...
Profit is not profit on paper alone.

There are two or three major divisions, or departments, in an average business. The first is *sales*, because nothing happens in any business until a sale is made. Without a sale there is nothing to administer, manufacture, develop, or fix. Then there is *administration*, which includes everything from financial management to human resources through purchasing, accounts receivable, and then some. And finally, we may have *manufacturing* or *product development*.

For the sake of this subject, we will not focus on manufacturing or product development, as these departments are not germane to turning promises into cash. And by promises I mean promises of orders into cold hard cash (or maybe it is soft warm cash) in the bank.

In the sales arena, it is a common mistake for sales personnel (and particularly upper management) to measure performance by the <u>sales numbers</u>. What if the selling price does not allow a profit after all expenses have been deducted because the salesperson cut the price to get the deal? The measurement of top performance is *gross margin dollars* generated from sales. I know your bank and investors and the shareholders and marketplace want to know your sales—and that is OK, but from an internal management point of view, it is gross margin dollars (GM$) that is the critical number, because GM$ minus expenses equals PROFIT. Would you rather have a business that sells $1,000,000 at 25 percent GM, or a business that sells $1,200,000 at 20 percent? Exactly!! Lower sales often generate more gross margin dollars. One business is viewed to be 20 percent bigger than the other because of sales <u>volume</u>, yet the smaller company is generating more GM$ (and because it is smaller, probably has a lower overhead), so consequently shows a greater <u>profit</u>.

The sale is made, the product delivered; now your customer owes you money. This is your Account Receivable (A/R), and you assume it is *collectable*, and that it will be collected *on time*. In reality this does not always happen.

There are two schools of thought in collecting overdue accounts. One is to have the salesperson (who has a relationship with the customer) try and help collect the outstanding amount. Some salespeople don't like this because they feel it may ruin their relationship with the customer. The other is the obvious one of leaving the collection in the hands of the A/R or Collections Department. My experience has shown me that a combination of the two works best. That is, let the first contact to the customer come from the salesperson, with whom they have a relationship. And only if this is unsuccessful, should the A/R Department step in. The A/R Department should be ever mindful that this account, though currently delinquent, will likely remain a customer in the long term, and they should therefore always be understanding and courteous, while still being firm in seeking a settlement of the account.

Each day that a receivable is overdue *lessens the chance of the account being collected*. If a customer is on thirty-day terms and the account goes past due to thirty-one days, then thirty-five days, the possibility of collecting the outstanding balance diminishes. To manage A/R well, it is imperative to intervene *immediately* when an account becomes <u>one</u> day overdue. Call your customer and simply <u>ask</u> what happened to the payment—are they delaying payment because of something your company may not have done for them—or do they have an internal reason for not paying. From there on, that customer should receive a call at least *every second day*. Remember the squeaky wheel gets the grease. And when payment is received, it should never be assumed the check will go through the bank; if the customer is on "credit hold," do NOT take them off "hold" until the check has cleared through the bank.

Some pointers that will help you succeed at making collection calls with positive results:

- Set aside a certain time of week for making collection calls.
- Sit up straight and SMILE, even though your customer cannot see you; this will increase your confidence and direct your attitude.
- If you must leave a voice message, state your name, company name and number, and request a call back. *Do not state the reason for your call*, as this will deter a callback.
- If you connect, simply *ask why* the payment has not been made…*then shut up and listen*.
- If there is a problem with the order, the product, delivery, back-order, etc.,—rectify it appropriately.
- If the customer admits an inability to pay, work out a payment plan but aim to collect as much as you can as soon as you can (e.g., 50 percent now, then two more payments of 25 percent each fairly soon after).
- If you are set up to do so, process the first payment immediately (e.g., credit card or check-by-phone).

- Be *very clear* what the arrangement is by having the customer repeat it back to you before you end the call.
- THANK the customer. You want to save the relationship.
- Follow-up the agreement in a letter or e-mail and stay on it.

***Dollars on the P&L don't count
if they don't make it to the bank.***

> "What gets measured gets done. What gets measured and fed back gets done well. What gets rewarded gets repeated."
>
> John E. Jones
> *Leadership Trainer*

COMMON SENSE MATTERS

On Leading

Measure Everything... *You can't manage it if you don't measure it*

OK, this is a truism…but you really **can't manage it if you don't measure it**, period.

The challenge is…what do you measure, and what do you do about it?

All good leaders and managers have **K**ey **R**esult **A**reas (KRAs), which are germane to their success. I cannot tell you here what your KRAs should be, but I can tell you, you need to have them.

Following is an example for a medium-sized business. Please understand, though, that you need to develop your own KRAs, ones that are important to <u>you</u>, as the leader.

From an altitude of 50,000 feet, depending on the size of your business, you probably want to know on a regular basis (at least, weekly):

- ➢ Sales Month To Date (MTD)
- ➢ Total Accounts Receivable (AR)
- ➢ Total Accounts Payable (AP)
- ➢ Cash on Hand

On Leading

All management positions have KRAs—only some managers don't realize it. Your CFO, Factory Manager, Sales Manager, in fact, even sales personnel need them—and I do encourage leaders to help managers within their companies to develop these KRAs and ensure they are measured on a regular basis (minimum weekly).

Choose whatever topics you feel are the most important for you. Here a three rules:

1. Review them first thing in the morning.
2. Do it at least every week—make it a habit.
3. **ACT ON THE INFORMATION**

Besides being able to anticipate problems, it gives you a golden opportunity to communicate with your employees. It may be an "Atta Girl," a question, or a reprimand—but everyone will know you have your eye on the ball.

What you need to do with your information or "diagnosis" depends on the challenges it brings to light. These are the symptoms that will you allow you to make an early diagnosis of any emerging ailments in the business. Use your KRAs to highlight areas where you can effect change on a short term basis. Use your monthly financial reports to effect change on a monthly basis.

Now that I have mentioned KRAs, it may be a good time to touch on *reporting* in general. Here are some questions that all leaders should address:

How frequently should you get reports? Operational and sales activities may need to be provided on a daily basis—which are the KRAs referred to above. On a weekly basis, items like cash flow, billable hours, etc., would probably suffice. However, at a minimum, the full financial results should be analyzed on a monthly basis.

How will you know it is accurate? Internally prepared reports <u>must</u> be accurate. If they are not, you have the wrong staff in place. There should be a consistency in all reports provided, e.g., earnings on job reports should be consistent with the profit on the income statement. The cash forecast should track with sales, payables, and receivables.

Why is consistency important? Consistency is critical. Getting important information once in a while just won't cut it. It will negatively affect your effectiveness in your business. The earlier a problem can be detected, the better equipped you team will be handle the issue.

Who should get the reports? Anyone responsible for the results should get the reports. Performance that is measured improves.

In the end, the reason you have a business is to make money. Yes, there are all the other nice things like team spirit, doing what you love, changing the world, and so on—but the bottom line is that you *need a bottom line* and it needs to be written in black ink and not red ink. If that doesn't happen, then everything else is academic. There is one rule that holds true for a one-man show or the government of the United States of America:

> *Expenses must be the slave of your revenue...*
> *not the other way round.*
> *Wouldn't it be great if governments realized this!!*

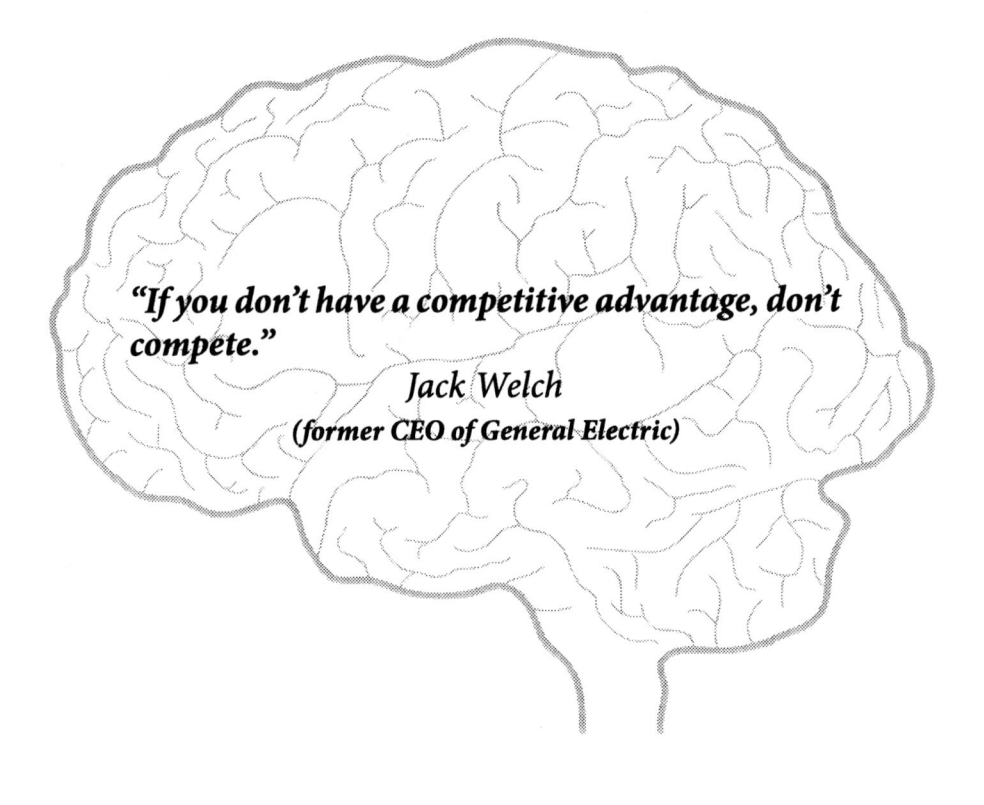

"If you don't have a competitive advantage, don't compete."

Jack Welch
(former CEO of General Electric)

COMMON SENSE MATTERS

On Leading

Create a Competitive Advantage...*Play to your strengths*

Below you will find five questions that you should answer if you want to learn your company's *competitive advantage*. However, there are a few rules you need to adhere to in answering these questions.

- **Firstly,** the competitive advantages MUST be quantifiable; they must NOT be clichés; and they must NOT be able to be claimed by your competitors.
- **Secondly,** special qualities must be very specific, meaningful, and persuasive to the customer.
- **And finally,** words like quality, knowledge, reputation, and trust are not valid answers.

  - Based on your position in your company and your customer base, what are your top three competitive advantages over your competitors? (Remember the rules above).
  - What do your customers think are the most important differentiators for you versus your competitors? Ask them.
  - What are the three key reasons potential customers do not buy from you?

- If a prospect asks you, "What are the three reasons why I should buy from you?" what would your answer be. <u>Please remember the rules above.</u>
- What products would your customers buy from you if you carried them in stock?

If you cannot answer the questions above, honestly and in detail, then get hold of your management team and go back to the drawing board.

Know your strengths and play to them!

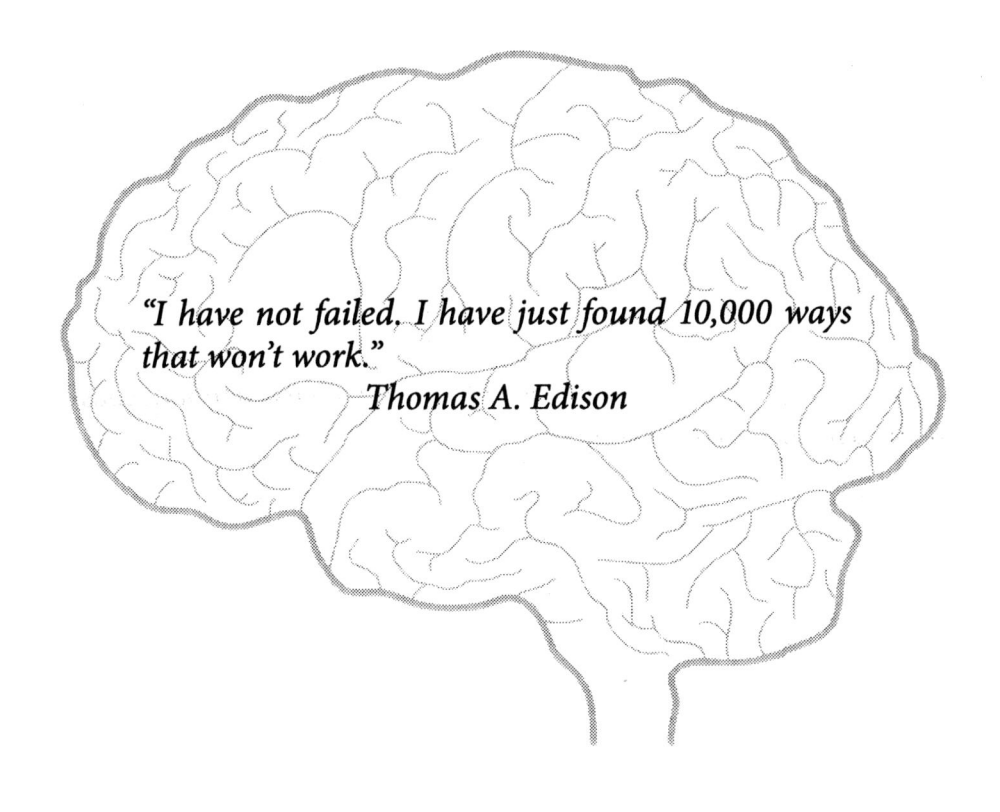

> "I have not failed. I have just found 10,000 ways that won't work."
>
> Thomas A. Edison

COMMON SENSE MATTERS

On Leading

Why Leaders Fail...Keep your eye on the "right" ball

Today's CEOs are four times more likely to get fired than a generation ago. Let's examine the reasons.

Sometimes learning *what not to do* teaches us more than *what to do*. In *Fortune Magazine*, Ram Charan and Geoffrey Colvin both made the following observation "After researching several dozen CEO failures over a couple of decades...70 percent of CEO failures are not because of the decisions they make, rather by the execution of these decisions."

Let's have a look at a self-test for leaders:

1. **Is your performance credible?** Leaders have to deliver results, but you will not be able to do this unless you have developed performance criteria for at least the next four quarters. You need to have ideas now on how you will change the performance criteria if the need arises anytime in the next four quarters. And when this quarter is over, add another quarter, so you always have four quarters' performance expectations.

2. **Are you focused on the basics of execution?** You should be connected to the flow of information about your company,

division, branches, etc., and its markets—that includes regular direct interaction with customers and frontline employees. Are you following through on all the commitments from your direct reports? And are you listening to that inner voice telling you whether things are going well or not?

3. **Marketplace problems** have to be taken seriously, acted upon, and reevaluated on a regular basis. Notwithstanding a SWOT analysis has been around for years, it often pays to revisit this formula to assess where you are in the marketplace. I have always found this analysis is best when the management team does it as a group exercise and every suggestion or idea is taken seriously. For the uninitiated, this is a measurement of **S**trengths, **W**eaknesses, **O**pportunities, and **T**hreats. Keep in mind when having a brainstorming session of this nature, no ideas are bad ideas. Every suggestion needs to be looked at with open mind.

Here is a brief example of a SWOT analysis:

<u>**S**</u>**trengths:**
- **We have talented personnel.**
- **We have a strong balance sheet.**
- **We are well established in our industry.**
- **We are profitable with a reasonably good cash flow.**

<u>**W**</u>**eaknesses:**
- **We do not have good geographical coverage.**
- **Various divisions of our company do not work as a team.**

- Our margins are slim, which makes us vulnerable.
- We have not grown as much as we could have because of our ultra-conservative outlook.

<u>O</u>pportunities:
- We can increase our footprint by expanding to other geographical areas.
- We can increase our revenue (and profit) by introducing additional complimentary, high margin, products to our product portfolio.
- Make a conscious effort to ensure greater cooperation between departments and divisions to foster a team environment, as opposed to a competitive one.

<u>T</u>hreats:
- A new, large competitor is moving into our primary marketplace.
- They are notorious for cutting price. And our margins are slim already.
- Complacency by our management because they believe we "own" the local market.
- Unless we manage our opportunities well, we may find we are in a cash flow squeeze while fighting our new competitor.

4. **Is your board or management team doing what it should?** That means evaluating <u>you</u> and your direct reports. Please know, if you don't want to be evaluated, it means you know you are not performing at the level you should.

a. Are your board or management team asking you difficult probing questions about your marketplace, your succession plan, your vision, etc.?
   b. Keep in mind, part of their job is to:
      i. probe your performance
      ii. manage their area of responsibility
      iii. they are *not to form strategy*—that is your job

5. **Is your own team discontented?** Remember top subordinates start bailing out before the leader goes down for the count.

Let us say after reading this you have some doubts about your performance. You have read the above and can't see yourself there. Are you doing OK, or are you simply a *denier*? Many major CEOs have bitten the dust because they denied the truth. Brilliant as some of them may have been, they acted like ostriches. Are you a closet denier? **Honestly** examine yourself against this checklist of traits that may signal you are in trouble:

1. Do you truly believe everything that is stated in your annual report?
2. Do you blame shortfalls on the weather, technology, or unfair competition?
3. Is your background restricted to sales and marketing?
4. Do your direct reports gripe about power issues, or corporate strategy—and leave?
5. Do you often make restructuring changes?
6. Do you load up your end of the month (or quarter) shipments to make profit targets?
7. Do you say you are a *realist*?

To summarize then, let us look at the profile of a superior CEO or leader:

1. **Integrity, Maturity and Honesty**—the foundation on which everything else is built.
2. **Business Acumen**—a deep understanding of the business and a strong profit orientation—an almost instinctive feel for how the company makes money.
3. **People Acumen**—judging, leading, growing, and coaching people—while possessing the strength to cut losses where necessary.
4. **Curiosity, intellectual capacity, and global mindset**—being externally oriented and hungry for knowledge of the world; adept at connecting developments and spotting patterns.
5. **Superior judgment**—Do you have the strength to be open-minded to any suggestions or criticisms you may get, yet still have the capacity to judge this input without prejudice.
6. **An insatiable appetite for accomplishments and results.**
7. **Powerful motivation to grow and to convert learning into practice.**

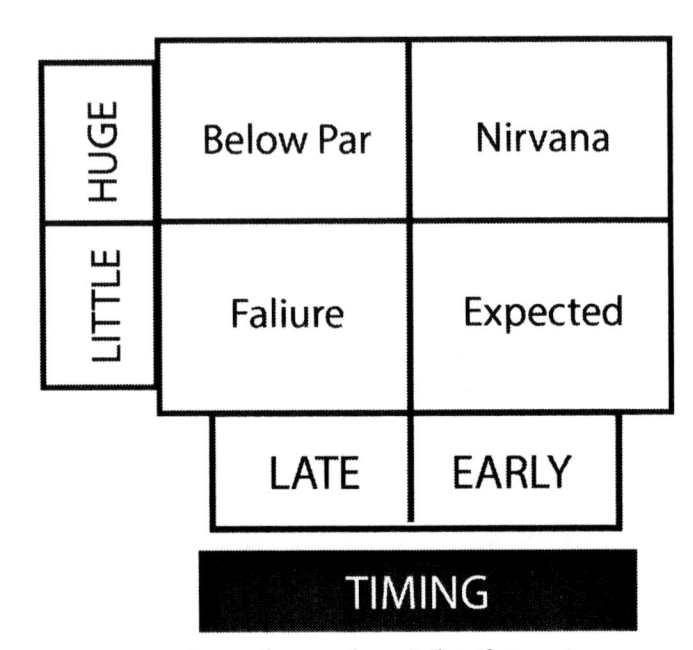

		Below Par	Nirvana
MAGNITUDE OF ACTION	HUGE		
	LITTLE	Faliure	Expected
		LATE	EARLY

TIMING

Are you worrying about the right things?

Execution
Decisiveness
Follow-through
Delivering on commitments

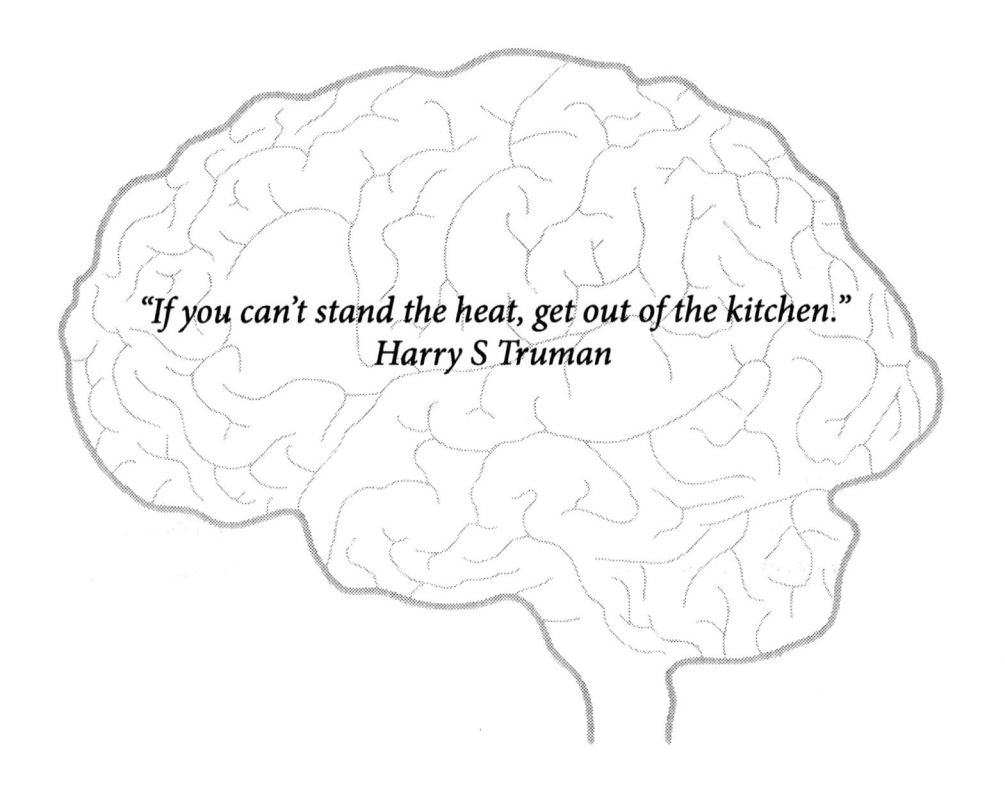

"If you can't stand the heat, get out of the kitchen."
Harry S Truman

COMMON SENSE MATTERS

On Leading

Leadership is Not for Everyone...*Step aside if you cannot step up.*

Leading is a tough job. As a leader, you have to make tough and unpopular decisions. You realize that you and your decisions will sometimes be criticized, both to your face and behind your back. This happens to every leader. Leaders who allow it to affect their decision making process do not deserve to be leaders. They should rather be a *number two* man / woman. Once a leader listens with an open mind to all relevant input, decision time comes. Pull the trigger. Take the consequences. And if you made a bad decision, make another decision to change the first one. If you can't do this—if you can't stand the heat, get out of the kitchen. Become a great number two instead of a weak number one.

There are far too many leaders in business who understand the theory of business but do not realize that when it comes to real life, the theory is sometimes very difficult to put into action. I have seen this on a regular basis with second or third generation leaders who believe they know what to do, but when it comes to pulling the trigger, the *intestinal fortitude* is not there.

For over twenty years, I have been a member of an international organization, formally The Executives Committee, now known as Vistage. Local chapters are typically composed of a group of ten to fourteen

CEOs who meet on a monthly basis to discuss problems and to listen to professional speakers. This is an international company with hundreds of groups worldwide. I clearly remember a meeting when one CEO posed the problem of having his brother-in-law performing well below the standard of what was expected of him, in the position he held. For four consecutive months, the group had offered him various solutions—he never acted on any of them. His excuse was always something like, what would the staff think, his wife would be angry, what would happen at family gatherings, etc. Suddenly, a member of the group said, "You do not deserve to be a CEO if you can't make hard decisions. If I was your boss, I would fire you, and in fact I do not want to be in the same group as you. You have no backbone." As a sidebar, the "weak CEO" resigned from the group and his company (now seven years later) is still below "mediocrity" and the brother-in-law is still employed there.

Let us look at Harry S Truman, thirty-third president of the United States, for a moment:

- *He had a simple sign on his desk that read "The Buck Stops Here."*
- *He dropped the A-bomb on Japan.*
- *He saved Europe from starvation.*
- *He kept the Soviets from enveloping Greece and Turkey.*
- *He rescued Berlin with the airlift.*
- *He halted the Communists in Korea.*
- *He integrated the military.*
- *He recognized Israel.*
- *He fired General McArthur.*
- *Yes, he fired General Douglas McArthur!*

- ***He delivered many times on his declaration, "The buck stops here."***

This man did what he believed was RIGHT. He took whatever heat was forthcoming. If you are a leader, have the same courage, and if you are a follower, find a leader that exhibits this kind of strength.

People responded to his courageous leadership, even if they did not always agree with him. During a campaign stop in St. Louis in 1950, someone in the crowd shouted, "Give 'em hell, Harry." It stuck as a nickname.

Later he declared that "I never gave anybody hell. I simply told them the truth and they thought it was hell."

COMMON SENSE MATTERS

ON SELLING

If no one sold anything to anyone, the world would come to a standstill.
Eric Levine

"You can have everything in life you want, if you will help other people get what they want."

Zig Ziglar
Motivational Guru

COMMON SENSE MATTERS

A Common Sense Observation on Selling

There are many different types of selling. There is retail-to-consumer selling, Internet-to-consumer selling, business-to-business selling, and many other permutations. Some of the Common Sense examples that follow may only apply to one or the other of these examples.

Please use your common sense as to which example applies to which target market.

COMMON SENSE MATTERS

Index of Thoughts on Selling...

Selling is a Profession... *A very unique profession* 201
The Critical Path... *The road to riches is paved with questions* 207
Managing Your Pipeline... *Moving a Prospect tobeing a Partner* 213
The Anatomy of a Sale... *The heart and lungs of a business-No Sales No Business* 219
What a Customer Values... *Solve their problems and the sale makes itself* 233
The Complex World of Social Media... *How the SM Revolution challenges business* 239
Always Be Marketing... *Your business needs business* 243
Keep Warm Program... *Keep the customer thinking of you* 245
Be Memorable... *Don't be just a face in the crowd* 251

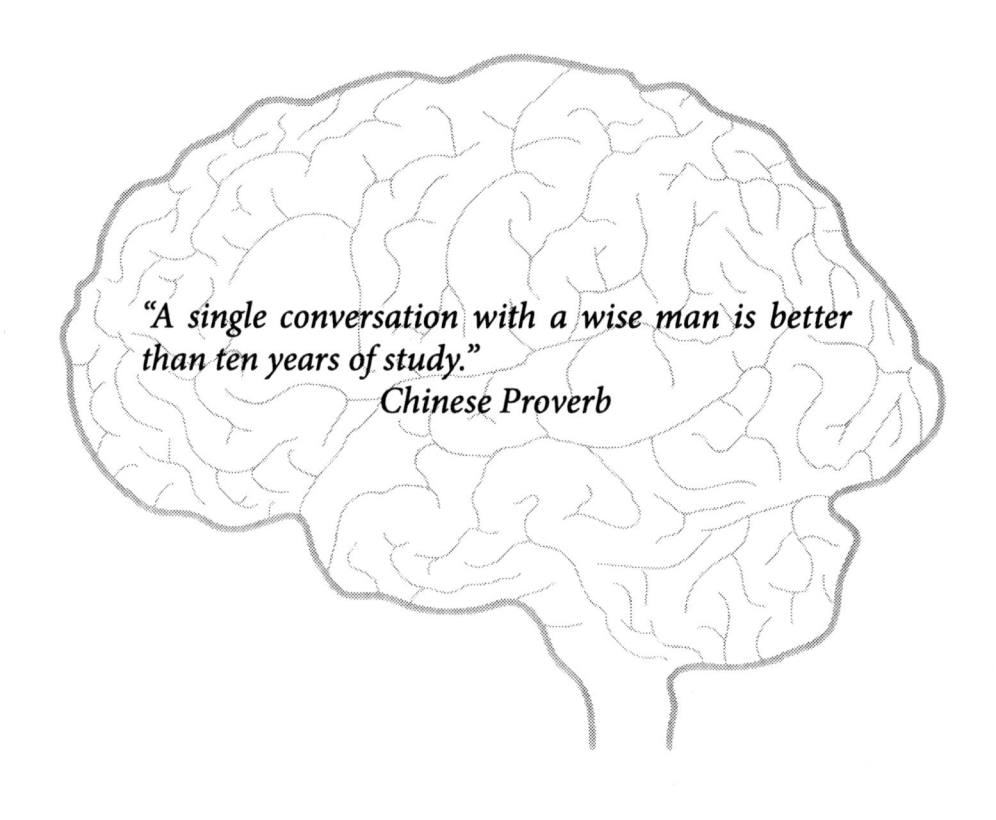

"A single conversation with a wise man is better than ten years of study."
Chinese Proverb

COMMON SENSE MATTERS

On Selling

Selling is a Profession!...*A very unique profession*

First we will take a look at some facts (and fiction) about selling as a *profession*. Then we will examine the ten **most dynamic principles** to which *a professional* salesperson must commit.

FACT—You don't need a college degree to be able to sell and be a professional salesperson.

FICTION—Anyone that has an outgoing personality and can tell a good joke can be good at selling.

FACT—It can be one of *the most expensive professions* from which to "graduate." If you were to calculate the commissions lost by any one salesperson because they erred in their selling presentation or technique, it would reach hundreds of thousands of dollars. Losing the sale on an average home could be upward of $20,000. If the average salesperson were to close one deal in four (a pretty fair average)—this would cost the sales person $60,000 per month in lost commissions. And that is easy to do in one month. *Talk about expensive tuition.* My son is a doctor, and the cost to make him a great doctor was nothing near that. There is also the cost to the company of the lost sales that needs to be considered.

On Selling

FACT—Yes, selling is a profession, with no college degree, with no cap and gown, with no diplomas—BUT with some of the **highest earning potential in the world**. And it is for this reason that so many people want to get into sales—but they are not prepared to pay the high price of LEARNING how to sell—and they don't realize it takes a heck of a lot longer to become proficient (never mind being a real pro) than a four-year college course.

FICTON—A pleasing personality will get you through.

There is a flip side to commission-based sales professionals for big-ticket items like homes, cars, boats, insurance, etc., and that is the salaried salesperson that works for a company selling a commodity, where the owner may not pay commission. There is a trade-off in this selling situation. This salesperson has greater job security but less earning potential. However, the need to be professional is not minimized because of the different selling environment. This sales person's upside is growth within their company and being sought after by competitors for bigger and better positions. Their security is their knowledge, their loyal customer base, and, of course, their confidence in their own *proven* ability.

Many salespeople and sales managers have fun trying to define selling. There is probably one definition for every salesperson out there. They range from:

- A. Taking a customer/prospect away from pain toward pleasure
- B. Trying to get your customer/prospect to feel about your product the way you do—so they *want* to own it
- C. Being able to tell a customer "to go to hell," and have them look forward to the trip

D. ………and many, many more
E. For me, I like to define selling as being able to fill a customer's needs and wants by helping them reach their goals, and always giving exceptional value, irrespective of what effort is required from me.

Now that we have established a framework for sales as a profession, let's examine TEN DYNAMIC PRINCIPLES to which every sales PROFESSIONAL must ascribe:

1. ***Believe* you can be a professional salesperson.** Learn, learn, learn. Believe in yourself and be PROUD of being a salesperson. If you have the attitude, "I took this selling job until I can find a real job," you are NOT a salesperson.
2. **Know your customers' *needs* and *wants*.** I want a Bentley convertible. I need a Chevrolet. What I should have is somewhere between the two, which will give me *quality of life* on the one hand, but on the other hand, will not exceed my budget. You discover your customers' wants and needs through *question-based selling*.
3. **Sell Value.** Paraphrasing John Ruskin's quote, "Someone will always sell it cheaper," so you have to bring something of value to the sale. Remember, for *your* price, the customer also gets YOU and all the fine edges your company has over the competition. Don't be shy to wear these advantages on your sleeve.
4. **Help customers buy.** People don't like to be "sold." But people like to "buy." I was once travelling with a salesman of mine, and he said to the customer, "Throw me a bone please; I'm with the boss." I nearly died of embarrassment. Remember, people buy from people. Be the person that can help your customer come to a good business decision—and you will always win.

5. **Be green and grow.** When you are green you will grow—when you are ripe you will rot! Always strive to improve and learn. I got a college degree at sixty-five. I am still trying to learn. Learn more about life, your profession, your family, anything—just keep on learning and growing.
6. **Know your product.** Know everything possible about the product you are selling. And if there is anything you don't know, NEVER wing it with a customer. Always offer to find the answer and get back to them ASAP.
7. **Know your competitors.** Know everything about your competitor and their products. Know what they're doing, when they're doing it. Know their range of products and pricing as well as you know your own. Stay current with their marketing programs.
8. **Great salespeople are "canned."** You do not need to make every presentation different. Great salespeople have a *winning formula* and they repeat it over and over again. It starts to be natural and will slide off your tongue easily, without sounding glib. If you are selling a commodity to a repeat customer, keep the same formula every time you see them, e.g., if they like to talk football before discussing business, then do it.
9. **What gets measured gets done.** Know every stat possible about your performance with every customer you have, as well as your overall performance. Know the number of calls per day, per week, per month. The same with closing averages (per customer as well). Know what product is being sold to what customers—when you lose a sale, know why. Measure every doggone thing you do and I guarantee your sales will improve dramatically.

10. **Tell it like it is, or you will show it crooked.** Be ethical. Be truthful. No BS—that is not what professional salespeople do. If I need to say more on this subject, then shame on you.

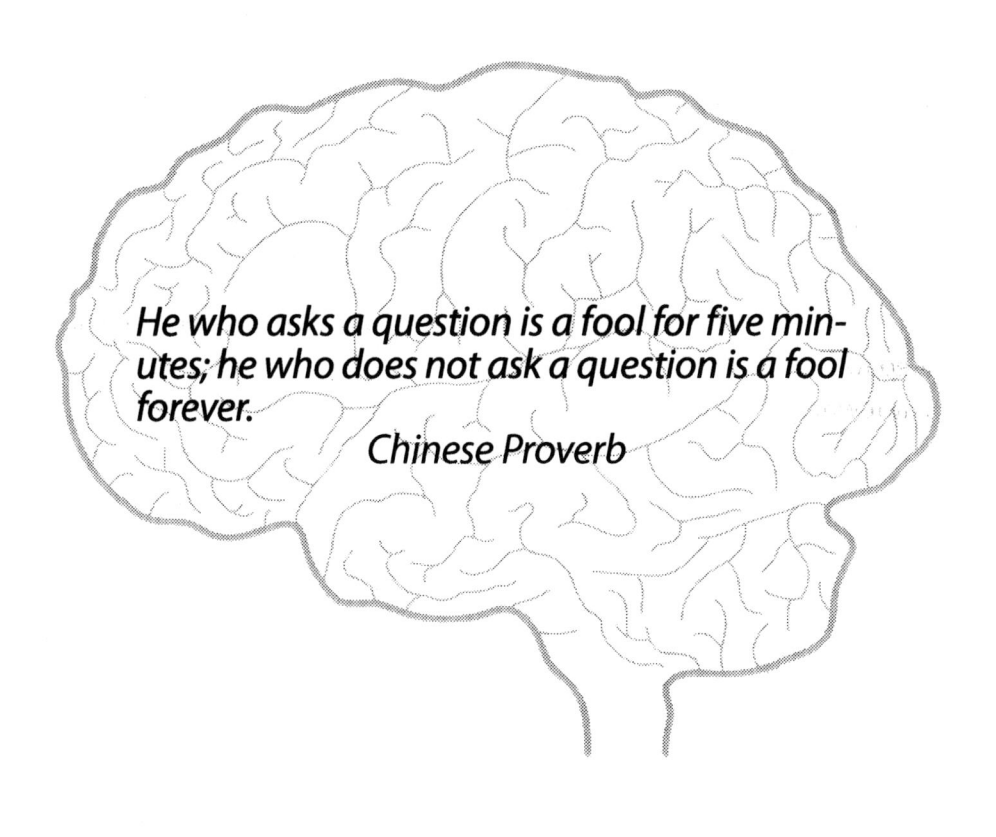

He who asks a question is a fool for five minutes; he who does not ask a question is a fool forever.

Chinese Proverb

COMMON SENSE MATTERS

On Selling

The Critical Path... *The road to riches is paved with questions*

I know some people who believe that sales training is not necessary. They believe that if you have a great personality and you are aggressive, then you will make a good salesperson. WRONG !! All that personality makes you is an enthusiastic amateur. If you want to be a PRO, then you need to know the right thing to do, all the time—and you need to know why it works. A great personality and a back-slapping, joke-telling attitude may work for the short term—but will not work for the long term.

> *I learned the question-based selling technique from an old TV talk show host—believe it or not!! In 1959, Jack Paar, who hosted the Tonight Show prior to Johnny Carson, interviewed the top sales trainer in America at that time, Og Mandino, who was in his early thirties. In the mid 1900s, Mr. Mandino was one of the first self-help authors to gain cultural acclaim. His bestselling book, The Greatest Salesman in the World, has sold over 50 million copies. Mr. Paar asked Og to sell him an ashtray that was on his desk. (In those days they smoked on TV). To cut a long story short, the discussion went something like this:*
>
> *"Mr. Paar, if you owned this ashtray, what would you use it for?"*

"As a receptacle for my cigarette ash and cigarette butts."

Og then asked, "If it could do that, what would you be prepared to pay for it?"

"One dollar," said Mr. Paar.

"Congratulations," said Og, "it's yours."

When Mr. Paar requested that Og give his advice on selling, he replied, ask the person what they want—then ask them how much they would be willing to pay for it—then it is your choice whether you will let them have it. And this, my friends, is the basis of question-based selling. So simple—so basic—so true. And TRUISMS ARE AGELESS.

The Critical Path to making a sale is made up of many small steps:

Question-based selling is the answer. Even when not selling, and simply having casual conversations with people, <u>ask questions</u>. It shows you are interested in the other person and the subject matter. It will help you build a relationship with the person and go a long way to having them like you—and we all like to be liked, don't we? Ask probing questions to find out the customers problems and needs. Probe. Probe. Probe. Do NOT jump into selling benefits until you fully understand the customers' problems or needs, as your benefits may not solve their problems or fill their needs.

God gave us two ears and one mouth, to be used in that proportion—so ask questions and listen to the answers. Don't only hear the words…listen to the music as well.

Tell the customer what you can do for them, by asking a question. For example, "If I did the following for you………, would this help solve your………problem?" This type of question forces an answer to be given to you. See the chapter on "The Anatomy of a Sale" to learn how to overcome the problem if the answer to your question is no.

If the answer is yes—ask for the order, i.e., ask a *closing question that confirms the customer has bought.* Remember that it may be required that you ask for the order numerous times before you get it. More business is lost by salespeople who are too scared to ask for the order than any other reason. And nine times out of ten, the salesperson won't ask for the order because they don't like to hear the word "no."

Help people buy—don't sell to them. People automatically put their guard up when they believe they are being "sold." You will have much more success if you help them "buy." This psychologically puts you on their side, as opposed to trying to get something from them.

Build Trust. Once a sale is made, and PAID for, you want to cultivate a relationship with your customer that will lead to many more sales. Continue to ask questions, LISTEN to their answers, and be their solution. This way you will EARN their TRUST. Once they TRUST you, they will continue to buy from you. You may want to think that a definition of selling is the "Transfer of Trust" from the seller to the buyer.

Shut-up and listen !!!!!! In any walk of life, the art of being able to listen is one of the greatest attributes you can have. This does not only apply to the field of selling, but in any walk of life. Whether it is a personal relationship, a business relationship, or even an argument—learn to listen. As I said before, don't just hear the words, but listen to the music as well. Here is how I made a $100,000,000 sale by doing just this (sitting and listening to a customer for two and one-half hours without uttering a word), and only asking two questions (*a la Jack Paar and Og Mandino*):

> NTT (Nippon Telephone & Telegraph in Japan) wanted a quote from my boss and me, to develop a billing software package for the Japanese telephone system. My boss told me the potential of the order was +/- $50,000,000. We went to Tokyo for the "presentation" and sat in front of a board of eight executives from NTT. When they asked us to give the presentation, <u>I asked my first question</u>. I said that I did not want to be presumptuous and assume I knew, or understood, their problems, so I asked if they would spell out for me what they needed before my presentation. This took them two and one-half hours. <u>Then came my second question to the board.</u> I asked them what they would pay if I could give them what it was they were looking for. Their response was quite adamant; they responded by saying, and this is close to being verbatim, "Not one penny more than $100,000,000—American." Remember, we were prepared to quote the program for $50,000,000. I asked if we could leave their offices and give them an answer at 8:30 the following morning. They said yes. The next morning I told the board that we felt there were certain aspects of the software package that they needed that they had not addressed, which would cost approximately $8,000,000 more—but seeing that their budget was only $100,000,000, we would do the entire package for that amount. <u>Then came the closing question.</u> "Would it be satisfactory to you if we delivered you phase one of the project in six months, with a guarantee the entire project would complete within eighteen months of the starting date?" They said yes. Then all we had to do was work out the wording in the contract. That's right, a $100,000,000 sale by just listening

and only asking two questions, and we sold the product for $50 million more than we were prepared to accept in the first place.

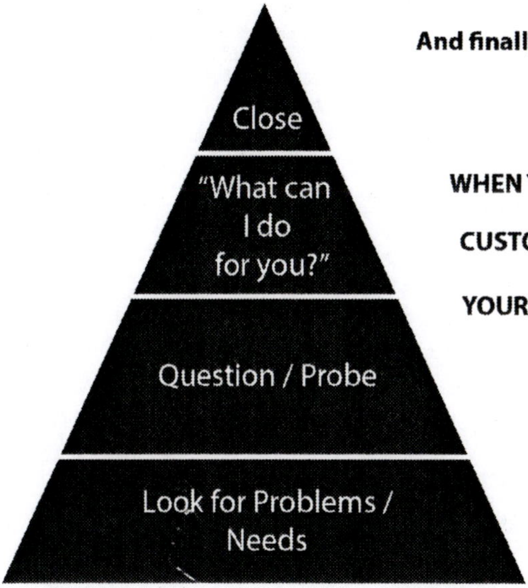
Close
"What can I do for you?"
Question / Probe
Look for Problems / Needs

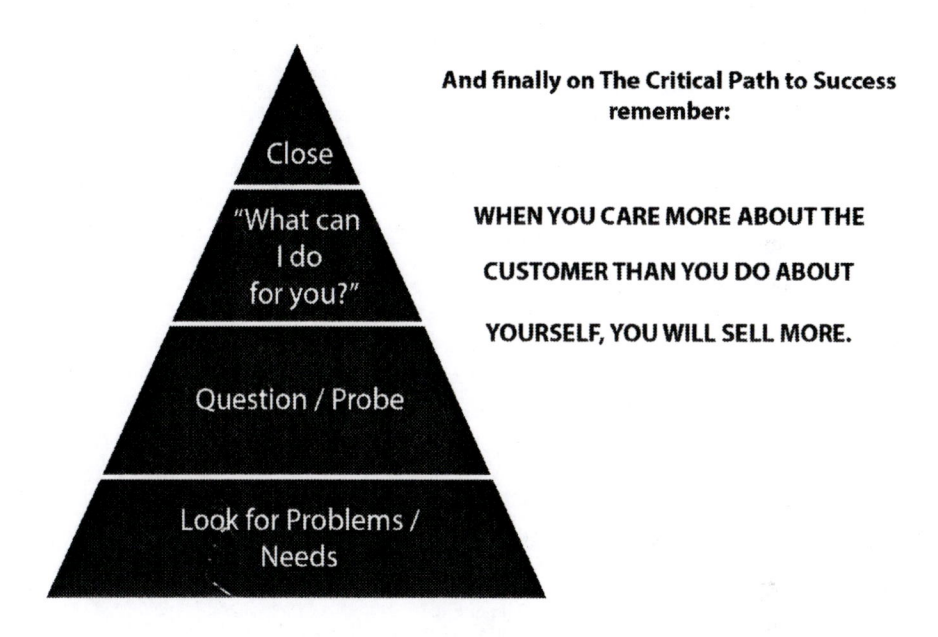

And finally on The Critical Path to Success remember:

WHEN YOU CARE MORE ABOUT THE CUSTOMER THAN YOU DO ABOUT YOURSELF, YOU WILL SELL MORE.

He who asks questions is in control of the conversation, in any walk of life..

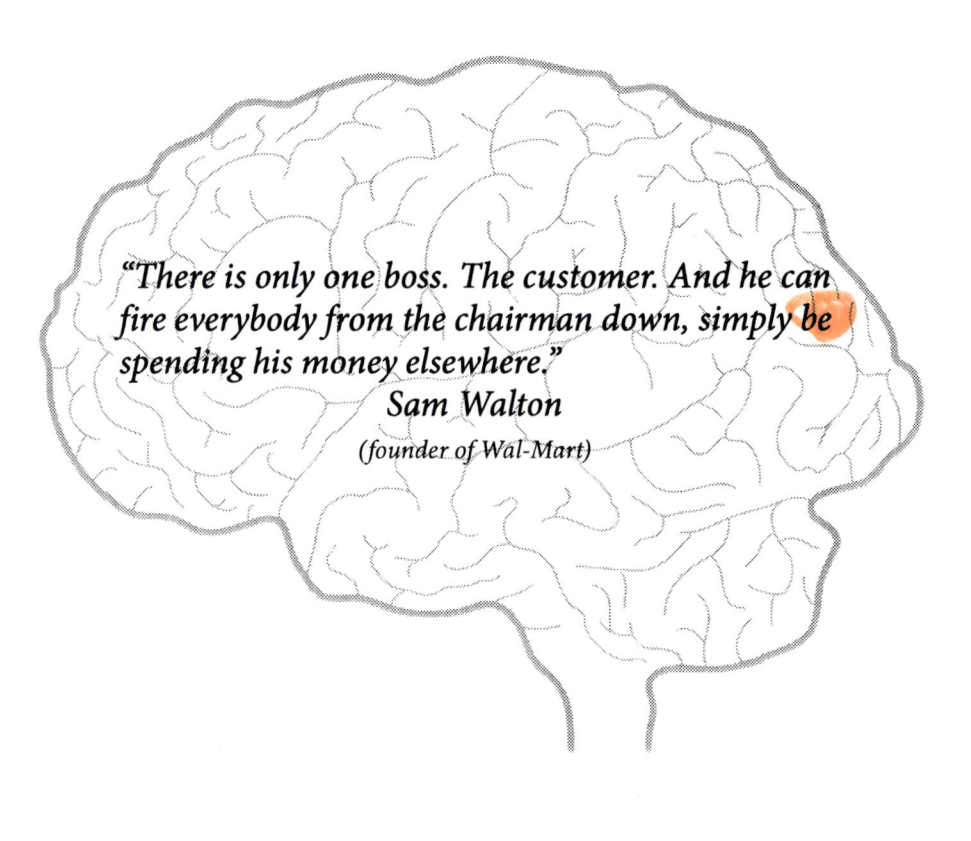

"There is only one boss. The customer. And he can fire everybody from the chairman down, simply be spending his money elsewhere."
Sam Walton
(founder of Wal-Mart)

COMMON SENSE MATTERS

On Selling

Managing your Pipeline…Moving a Prospect to being a Partner

There are five stages to what we commonly call a *customer*. I believe we don't simply want a customer—we want and deserve more. Let's take a look at the progression of these stages:

1. **We start off by having a *suspect*:** someone that we haven't even spoken to that we think may one day become a customer. A suspect is more commonly referred to as a lead. We find leads from trade shows, purchasing lists, local directories in print and online, and we get leads from our best source, *referrals. A suspect in consumer-direct selling is anyone who reads a newspaper ad, watches a TV ad, or surfs the net.*
2. **Then we graduate to having a *prospect*:** someone we have spoken to that may be interested in doing business with us—but who is not yet buying from us. Someone who walks into your store looking for what you advertised is a prospect.
3. **Now we come to that beautiful thing we call a customer**: But hang on a minute—if someone buys from us once we call them a customer. Great. If they never buy again they are still on our books as a customer. Is this really what we want, or is there a possibility to take them to the next step?

4. **We are getting to where we want to be. We now have a *client*:** A client is someone that keeps coming back to us and gives us a continuous stream of business (or leads). We are solving their problems, we are HELPING them buy, we are building TRUST.
5. **Then we reach Nirvana. We have a *partner*. This is a particularly relevant scenario in a B-to-B relationship.** A partner is a client who would recommend their brother to do business with us. This is a client who gives us the lion's share of their business and understands that <u>we bring *added value* to their business by doing business with us.</u> This is a client that does not quibble over pennies or threaten to bolt to our competitors. This is a client who lets us into their business and openly discusses problems with us, and asks for our help with solutions.

Now, each of the five groups above need to be managed differently, depending on your industry, when they are your in our pipeline—even though the philosophy behind managing them is the same. The underlying premise in managing a pipeline is on how many times you *touch* your customer, and how you touch them.

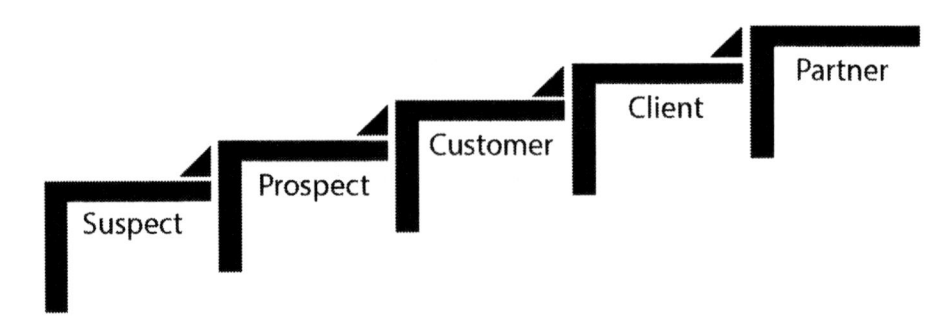

Suspect → Prospect → Customer → Client → Partner

Let's look at some examples:

Suspect: The objective of speaking to a suspect is to determine whether or not they are potential customers. In a B-to-B situation, this normally should be done by visiting them, so you can ask relevant questions that are nonthreatening. If you cannot determine their potential in two visits, you are asking the wrong questions. But, as I said, a lot of initial contacts with suspects are done by phone. Particularly if you are in a B-to-C business. This requires a lot of practice and expertise. Ensure you know the questions you are going to ask. Make sure the questions do not sound threatening—also be sure it doesn't sound like you are reading the questions. Speak clearly and slowly so the potential customer does not have to ask, "What was that you said?"

Prospects: Once a suspect has graduated to being a prospect, you should always have them on record. "Things" change. Prospects get disenchanted with their current supplier! The market changes! You get a broader range of products! Never stop touching them! A touch could be a visit, a phone call, a postcard, an e-mail, a tweet, or any other form of communication. If you are not getting business from them, then over time you may touch them less frequently, but always be touching them. A great idea to stay in touch with them, and to show them you care, is to find an article of interest to them, in any magazine or newspaper, and send it to them, with a comment on the article. And you **WILL** know what to send them, because you asked them the **RIGHT** questions when you visited them. When you next see them, you will be accepted so much better.

Customers: Unless you are getting all the business humanly possible from a customer, you have to keep striving to do more business with them. As new products come on board, or new services become available, you will know which customer will benefit from these as solutions to their challenges. BE their resource so you can increase your sales.

(Please see the section on "Keep Warm Program (KWP), for more in-depth details on Pipeline Management for Customers, Clients, and Partners)

"The best of merchandise will go back to the shelf unless handled by a conscientious, tactful salesman."

James Cash Penney
(Entrepreneur, founder J.C. Penney stores)

COMMON SENSE MATTERS

On Selling

The Anatomy of a Sale...*the heart and lungs of a business. No sales...no business.*

What you see below is a diagram that separates the good from the great, the enthusiastic amateur from the pro, a true method that will put the "fun" into selling and help you close more deals. But you need to follow this formula without wavering, and remember, this takes practice and more discipline than you can imagine.

> ***When learning <u>any</u> new process or procedure you must have patience. Remember the positive takes time. Only negative "stuff" happens quickly.***

Let's look at how this works:

Introduction: The introduction is simply breaking the ice. It is *small talk* that may introduce you to the prospect or a hale and hearty question to a client about something you may have discussed previously. Don't make the introduction too long, but on the other hand, don't be too abrupt. Adapt your personality to suit your audience.

ON SELLING

Anatomy of a Sale

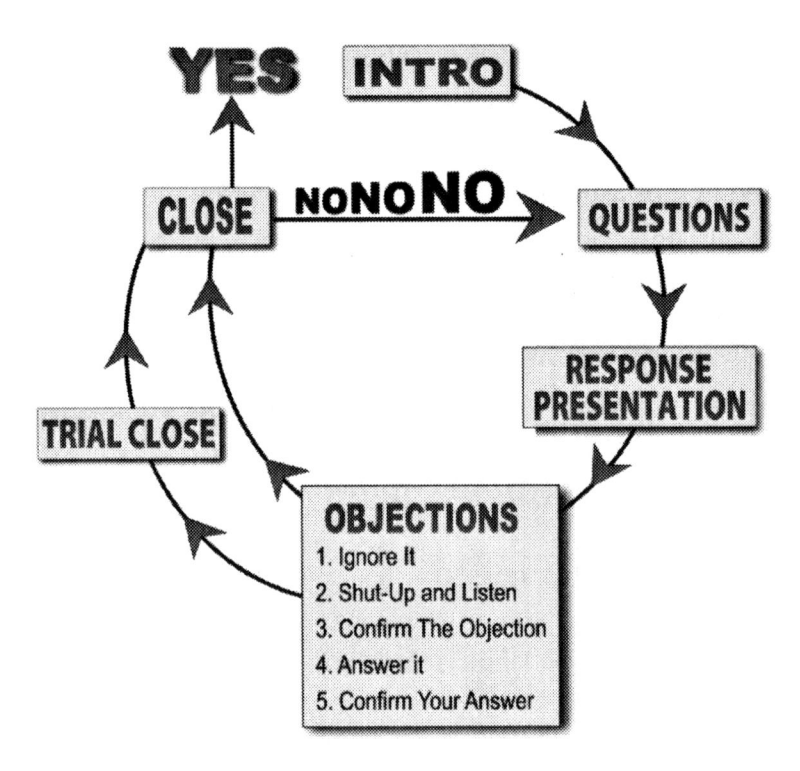

```
           YES ── INTRO
            ↑        ↓
   CLOSE ── NoNoNO → QUESTIONS
    ↑                    ↓
    │              RESPONSE
    │              PRESENTATION
    │                    ↓
   TRIAL CLOSE ←── OBJECTIONS
                   1. Ignore It
                   2. Shut-Up and Listen
                   3. Confirm The Objection
                   4. Answer it
                   5. Confirm Your Answer
```

Questions: Question-based selling is taking the customer by the hand and gently finding out what their needs and challenges are—then discussing with them solutions to their problems. **This is an art form.** Seriously!! In any selling situation there are probably a minimum of twenty generic questions that could be asked of the potential buyer—and this is where the art, learned by experience, comes in—only ask questions that take you one step closer to being able to ask for the order and do NOT ask all the questions in your arsenal at once. Let me share with you an example of a question for B-to-B selling and a method you can use if you are calling on a prospect. "Mr. Prospect, what would you like to see your current vendors do better than they are currently doing?" Or for a B-to-C customer, a question could be, "When looking to own (never use the word "buy," people don't want to be buyers, they want to be "owners") a home, what features are most important to you?"

LISTEN to the answer. Now, irrespective of the answer, **DO NOT JUMP IN AND SAY, "WE CAN DO WHAT YOU REQUIRE,"** or something similar. Simply respond by saying, "I understand." You will be using this response to your advantage as the interview progresses.

Here are some examples of questions that you can ask **prospects/customers:**

- Who is your primary vendor?
- Why do you use them?
- What do they do to bring VALUE to your business?
- Where do you see your business this time next year?
- What is your current vendor doing to help you get there?
- What do you need to do to get there?

Here are some examples of questions that you can ask existing B-to-B **customers:**

- How is business?
- Do you believe you should be doing better?

- What is preventing you from doing better?
- May I share with you how I think I may be able to help?

Here are some examples of questions that you can ask **whales (high rollers; big players):**

- What is your major challenge in today's business environment?
- Are you achieving the goals you have set for your business?
- How does your primary vendor add VALUE to your business?
- How does your primary vendor help you solve business problems?
- May I share with you how I see our relationship, and how I may be able to help you by adding greater VALUE to your business?

Remember that in any conversation you may have in life, be it selling, business, or social:

"He who asks the questions is in control of the conversation."

Once you have asked enough questions to feel confident that you understand the customers' needs and that you can truly help them, you enter into the response section of "The Anatomy of a Sale."

Response: In a conversational way, you now refer back to the responses you got to some of your earlier questions. For example, to your previous question you would comment, "Mr. Prospect, remember when I asked you what you would like to see your current vendors do better, and you mentioned that, since you were on outskirts of the city, you always tended to get your deliveries at the end of the day? Well, I do think it is worth mentioning that our Standard Operating Procedure (SOP) is that orders placed before 4:00 p.m. will be delivered before noon the following day. Is that the kind of delivery service that would make your life easier?" (You know the answer has to be "yes.") This is another question taking you closer to the close—*and by asking the question, you REMAIN IN CONTROL.* After four or five of these exchanges, you will be ready to close.

But, oh my, that is way too easy. Now, you get zapped with an…

Objection: What you want is to determine the TRUE objection because this brings out the Predominant Buying Motive (PBM) of the customer. This is where you must exercise discipline. There is a formula *to which you must adhere* if you want it to work. Once again, remember it takes patience and practice to perfect a new process. I reiterate, the positive takes time—only the negative happens quickly.

1. **Ignore the objection the first time it is brought up.** This is because everyone believes they must object to "being sold"—that it is their obligation to say "no." If it is a valid objection, they will bring it up again, and you will handle it then. So, when you first get the objection, simply say, "I understand," and move on. Then, if the objection gets brought up a second time…

2. **Shut up and listen—and don't interrupt until the prospect is finished explaining their objection.** When the prospect is finished…

3. **Confirm and clarify the objection.** "Just so I understand you correctly, sir, the only problem you have with our product that is preventing you from giving us your business is that we offer a three-year guarantee versus the five-year guarantee that you prefer. Is that correct, sir?" <u>Another question—and you stay in control while clarifying the objection</u>. Then, when you get a "yes"…

4. **Answer it. State clearly and truthfully** how **you can solve the problem, the objection, presented.** Once you answer the question, then…

5. **Confirm the answer.** *Be absolutely sure you ask this question:* **"That answers your question, doesn't it sir?"** Now one of two things happen:

6. Either the customer says "no," in which case you will have to ask probing questions again to ferret out the real objection (the PBM)…

7. Or the customer says "yes"—in which case you ask a *closing question.*

We all know the objection a salesperson gets more than any other is, "Your price is too high,"—or some connotation of this sentence. This is why you have to add VALUE and why <u>you need to get your customer to understand the difference between</u> <u>price and cost</u>. Price is what the customer initially pays for the product. Cost is the total cost of the product for the duration of its usefulness—including repairs, spares, etc. So, if the price of a product is $300 and it lasts for five years, its cost is $60 per year (excluding repairs, etc.). If the competitive product's price is $250, but its life expectancy is four years, its real cost is $62.50 per year.

An additional caveat here: If the customer is comparing your price to what the product can be purchased for on the Internet, point out that hidden costs like shipping, reduced warrantees, installation, delivery delays, lack of technical assistance, etc., could very well eradicate any savings.

Closing the sale: When closing a sale, there are two routes you can go. If you are a strong closer, you use the closing techniques that you have most success with, e.g., the alternate choice close, the negative yes close, the puppy dog close, etc. We'll get to those in a moment.

If you are not a strong closer, use a **Trial Close,** which asks for an opinion, as opposed to asking for the buying decision, e.g., "If you were to own this widget, where would you put it?" Then whatever answer you get automatically confirms that (mentally/subconsciously) the customer has "bought."

If you can't close the sale on this attempt (refer back to "Anatomy of a Sale" chart) you must start asking questions again, and again, and again.

The customer can say "no" ten times—but <u>only has to say "yes" once</u>, and you have won.

You have to learn *closing questions* if you want to be successful in selling. The definition of a closing question is a question you ask the prospect, the answer to which confirms he has bought. As I have always said, "There is no such thing as a great salesman. There are only great CLOSERS."

The more sales you close, the sooner you will develop a closing instinct that works for <u>you</u>. Then you will only need two or three closing attempts instead of the normal six or seven.

There is only one way to develop a closing instinct:

> *"Close too soon, too often, rather than too late, too seldom."*

There are probably more than twenty-five practiced closing questions/techniques used by pros. Here are just a few—keeping in mind you can use the same type of close in numerous ways.

The "Assumptive" Close

This is a closing technique every salesperson must have in his/her inventory, as it will probably be used in 90 percent of your sales. It is also referred to as the **"Last Close."** As the name indicates, it assumes the customer has bought.

You take out your order pad or tablet and ask,
- "What address do want the product delivered to?"…or
- "What is the P.O. number?"…or
- "Are there any special delivery instructions?"

You can use an incomplete sentence with the same effect.
- "And you want it delivered on…(pause)?" If they tell you, then they have bought.
- "And want it delivered to…(pause)?" If they tell you, then they have bought.

All these questions are assuming the customer has bought. Therefore, any answer will confirm the customer has bought.

The "Alternate Choice" Close
When using this closing technique, give the customer a choice of two, *only two*, options; either answer will confirm she has bought.

- "Would you like it delivered on Monday or Tuesday?"
- "Seeing it's still early, I can get it to you this afternoon, or would you prefer it tomorrow?"
- "Do you want billing terms, or should we charge your card?"
- "So do you want the T115 or the T135 model?"

A certain young man called my daughter numerous times and asked her to go out on a Saturday night. She really happened to be busy. But she wanted to go out with him, and she was worried he would stop calling. She asked for my help. I taught her the reverse Alternate Choice Close—so when he next called, she told him she was busy the following Saturday night, but could go out with him on Sunday or Friday. He immediately jumped at the chance and gave her a day. It didn't matter what he said—she had a date—or rather, "closed the sale." If her date had known how to close, he would have asked her an Alternative Choice Close and saved both of them some embarrassment. Can you make it Friday or Saturday night?

The "Negative Yes" Close
Some people love to say "no." So let them—but make the "no" mean "yes, I want to buy."
"Tell me, Mrs. Jones, I can see you are of two minds whether or not you want to make a decision now. May I ask:

- "Is it because you don't trust what I have told you about the product?" Answer is "no."
- "Is it because you don't think we can deliver as promised?" Answer is "no."
- "Is it because you think the warrantee is invalid?" Answer is "no."

But every time the customer says "no," they are stating a reason to buy. Now you would proceed to the "Assumptive Close" or the "Alternate Choice Close."

The "Emergency" Close

"Hey, Mr. Johnson, I know you are sitting on the fence about bringing some of these into your store, even though you realize they will bring you additional profit if you get them before the pending price increase. But if you were to get some in, how many would you want (Trial Close)?"

The customer's response could be, "If I were to get them, I would get six—but I'm not sure if I want them yet."

"May I just call my boss, please?"

"Hey boss, Mr. Johnson may want six widgets. Oh! OK! They're selling out fast. Hmmmm. Let me ask him, sir, hold on."

"Mr. Johnson, my boss says they are moving out of the warehouse quickly and we only have four in stock as we speak. Can I reserve them for you before we are all sold out, and our next delivery could be at a higher price?" If you get the right answer, you would proceed to the "Assumptive Close" or the "Alternate Choice Close."

The "Inflation" Close
This close is the same as the "Emergency Close"—only using a different base, i.e., the Emergency Close relates to being out of stock, whereas the Inflation Close relates to a pending price increase.

The "Door Knob" Close
When you have battled to get a "yes" but have failed to do so because you simply cannot get to the _real objection_, you tend to get exasperated and frustrated. So try this on for size:

Close your tablet or folio. Say good-bye and work your way to the door. Just as you get there you turn and say, "Bert, you know I really screwed up today, and I'm sorry."

"What do you mean?"

"Well, I really believe this product can make you money. And I have not been able to convince you—so I sort of feel like I let you down. Tell me where did I go wrong so I don't make the same mistake when I see the next customer?"

"Well, the product only has a two-year guarantee."

"WOW! I'm sorry; my mistake. I can't believe I neglected to mention our alternative three-year guarantee."

You now have the true objection, and you are in again.

The "Third Party" Close
This is a dynamic technique for an order you simply cannot nail down.

"Joe, I simply don't know if can offer you this deal, but if I can get my boss to OK (early delivery, cheaper price, extended terms, quantity discount, etc.), will we have a deal?

<u>Get the commitment up front!!!</u> If they don't give you the commitment, this is not the real objection—you MUST get them to say "yes." When asking a closing question like this, lower your voice, speak softly (non-threatening), and lean slightly forward in your chair. This body language will increase your closing probability five-fold.

Then call your manager AND LET YOUR CUSTOMER HEAR YOU SAY, "Hey boss, listen, I am with Joe at Joe's Pool Store, and I know you said no quantity discounts this month—but I really want to help Joe. He is loyal and he is committed to us—but I need to offer him a quantity discount. No, I promise I won't offer this to anyone else. Yes sir!! Thank you sir! Joe will really appreciate this."

When you put the phone down, where can Joe go when you say, "Joe, great news, the boss must be in a good mood. He said because of your loyalty over the years he feels it's time to show you that we do appreciate your business. Now you would proceed to the "Assumptive Close" or the "Alternate Choice Close."

The "Puppy Dog" Close

The way to sell a puppy dog is to leave it with the customer overnight. So, if your product is one that can be left overnight (or if there is some other way they can experience the benefit of the product in the short term), use this close.

Common Sense Matters

*You can be taught <u>how</u> to close, but no one can teach you <u>when</u> to ask a closing question—you can only get a **Closing Instinct** by <u>closing too soon, too often—rather than too late, too seldom.</u> I cannot stress this enough!*

"Don't sell life insurance. Sell what life insurance can do."

Ben Feldman

(American businessman, one of the most prolific salespeople in world history, sold $1,800,000,000 of insurance policies for New York Life)

COMMON SENSE MATTERS

On Selling

What a Customer Values... Solve their problems and the sale makes itself

As we learned in the last chapter, it is always important to distinguish between price and cost. The price of a product can always be higher than a competitor's—but in the long run, their product may cost more to maintain. This would make its price less, but its cost more. The following observation, not by some modern-day sales guru, but by Victorian-era British writer and professor John Ruskin, is as true today as it was then. **"There is no product that another man cannot make a little worse, or a little cheaper. The person who only buys on price alone is this man's lawful prey."**

So we have to offer *value. But what does a customer value*?? The answer will vary a bit by customer, but here are some indispensable tips for value-based selling:

- **GET PERSONAL**. Notwithstanding you are making a sales call, don't jump in the deep end immediately. Always refer to a previous conversation you had with the customer, and ask a few questions about what may have transpired. As an example, my wife had cancer and survived. If a vendor visits with me, I always appreciate it if they ask how my wife is doing. Kids have football games; find out what happened at Friday night's game...you get the picture. **Ask something personal.**

- **LET THE CUSTOMER KNOW YOUR TEAM.** What is your relationship to the Technical Department, to the Marketing Department, to your boss, to the company's support staff? It is imperative that the customer know you are not an island, and that you have a solid support around you. **Sell the corporate family, the team.**

- **CULTIVATE THE GATEKEEPER.** If you are selling B-to-B, she/he can be your greatest ally or your worst nightmare. Know their name (and use it). Know their "hot buttons."

- **FLY UNDER THE RADAR.** If you can't get to see the boss for some reason, like an overenthusiastic gatekeeper—work around her. For example, if he is a builder...
    - See what he builds.
    - Make it your business to meet the superintendent. Talk product to him. Talk benefits to him. He will respect you and your concern. And you can bet he will tell his boss. The guy you want to see—the decision maker. This way you get in "under the radar."

- **GO WITH THE *BEST*.** If you are always encountering the price objection with a customer, show them how to build value by asking them a simple question, **"Don't you want to give your customer the best possible product to fill their needs?"** It is very difficult for them to answer this question in the negative. I love this *statement-que*stion combination as it can be used during a price objection as well: "Mr. Jones, when a company goes into business, it has two choices in its approach to its customers. It can do as little as it can get away with (and we have all encountered these guys)—or it can do as much for you as is humanly possible. What is it you want me to do for you, sir, as much as possible or as little as I can get away with?" This indicates <u>they</u> are going with the best, and in the case of overcoming a price objection, what answer do you think you will get?

- **STAY ABOVE THE FRAY.**
    - **Don't gossip.** If you gossip, your customer will believe you do the same about them.
    - **Don't talk about their competitors.** This is a first cousin to gossip. If your customer wants to know about a competitor, let them ask, then answer the question in as few words as possible, and never slam or boast about their competitors. The same applies to talk about YOUR competitors.

- **YOUR WORD IS YOUR BOND.** Never ever do or say anything that could remotely compromise your **Integrity.** Ensure that you do what you say you will do, <u>every time</u>. You bring value to your relationship with your customer if he knows that he NEVER has to question your word, because you can rest assured he does not feel that way about all your competitors.

- **LEARN HOW TO MANAGE MONEY.** It is amazing how many bosses of small and medium-size companies do not have great expertise in managing money. Learn how to read financial statements, and remember that customers very often need guidance in managing money. Many businesses are forced to close even though they show paper profits—but don't know how to manage cash flow. I have a philosophy that drives my accountants crazy. I know I am academically wrong—but I am right at the same time. I don't care what the Profit and Loss statement says (within reason, of course)—if I have money in the bank, I am showing a profit. If I don't have money in the bank, I am showing a loss. Learn how to manage cash flow. This will give you an all-important part of the expertise needed on **how to manage a business. This will take you on the road to being a PRO. It will take you out of the role of being "just a salesperson." You will become a well-rounded professional. A business advisor. A product professional, and really a trustworthy friend.**

- **TALK ABOUT HOW TO MANAGE A BUSINESS.** Talk about marketing. Talk about customer service. Talk about turning inventory to improve cash flow. Talk about managing receivables. Talk about the value of partnering with vendors, staff, and customers…and so on…and on…and on.

- **BRING GREAT PRODUCT KNOWLEDGE.** Know your product inside out, backward and forward. Know what it can do and know what it can't do. Know how it compares to similar competitive products in the market. Know WHY it is better.

- **TEACH THEM TO SELL.** If you are selling B-to-B, teach your customers how to sell specific products to their customer (the consumer) through question-based selling.

- **DON'T BE A BORE.** Mind your voice intonation. Don't speak in a monotone. Talk about subjects in which they have an interest, etc., etc.

- **TOUCH EVERY CUSTOMER AT LEAST ONCE A MONTH.** See the chapter on the Keep Warm Program.
    - Remember, donuts don't cut it with the boss, **value does!!!** (but donuts can work well for their staff).

- If you are selling B-to-B, let this be your *pièce de résistance*—call ten customers every Friday morning before 9:00 a.m. and ask them, **"Is there anything I can deliver today so you can hit the ground running on Monday?"**

I guarantee you will close 50 percent of these calls.

> "If you make customers unhappy in the physical world, they might tell six friends. If you make customers unhappy on the Internet, they can each tell 6,000 friends."
>
> *Jeff Bezos*
> *(CEO, Amazon.com)*

COMMON SENSE MATTERS

On Selling

The Complex World of Social Media... *How the SM Revolution challenges business*

Where should social media fit in life, or leading, or selling? It is applicable to all three...so let's examine here how you can apply it wherever you wish.

For all of social media's disruptive qualities, one might ultimately stand out above all others: *It is fundamentally changing the way the world communicates.*

Take the business world for example. Whether through public social media like Facebook, Twitter, and LinkedIn—or social platforms for business like Salesforce.com or Chatter, social media has infiltrated the workplace and injected more interactions with more business contact than ever—broadcasting for all, or many, to see worker titles, responsibilities, areas of expertise, recent projects, and much more.

The platforms might change, but social media figures to be a fixture in business settings for the foreseeable future. We will have social media in just about every walk of our lives for generations to come. Social media may be the way for businesses to flatten their organizations in the ways Peter Drucker, business author, consultant, and philosopher, had envisioned. The world of selling, and inter-vendor-to-customer relationships now has an added dimension that will give the astute user a jump on the competition. JetBlue Airways is a great example of how to keep employees "in the know" by using SM as a medium to keep them informed about company happenings as well as how they connect with coworkers. With all the social media platforms we have today, we can anticipate more and more people (and companies) using Facebook, LinkedIn, Twitter, and the like—however, unshackling employees from using the over-two-decade-old e-mail will be hard. Michael Stelzner, CEO and founder of the Social Media Examiner blog, points out that there are many more personal business communication benefits in SM than e-mailing. For instance, gone are the days when workers, salespeople, executives and vendors have to have an associate's contact information that causes getting this information to become a laborious project. Today, if they have a person's name, chances are that they can find them on one of the social networks.

And the scary thing is that today we are in the embryonic stages of social networking. So we all need to educate ourselves as much as possible, as quickly as possible, not only to be ahead of the game—but to simply stay in the game.

> "The distinctions between advertising and marketing are blurring, requiring new roles and new forms of **consumer-centric** marketing."
>
> *Dr. Saul Berman*
> *IBM Global Business Services*

COMMON SENSE MATTERS

On Selling

Always be Marketing... *Your business needs business*

I don't understand why companies, when referring to their Sales/Marketing Departments, say, "Sales and Marketing." Here we have two completely different disciplines with completely different skill sets being lumped together. And what is more of an anomaly is that it is always "Sales & Marketing," and never "Marketing & Sales." Yet normally in a business, the marketing effort comes first—to create a demand—and the sales follow.

Marketing should be an activity that never stops in a business. Your business needs business, so don't skimp on marketing. Good marketing is not a support mechanism for sales; good marketing will make sales happen. The really big hurdle often tends to be funding. You have to spend on marketing. It creates a big lump in your throat if you are in a startup business or cash is tight; I understand that. What you must do to start getting a decent return on your investment is to start picking the "low hanging fruit" in your market; target it and market to it. There are volumes of excellent resources dedicated to marketing theories, practices, and methods. Suffice to say here that marketing is an unequivocal necessity in any business at any stage of its lifecycle.

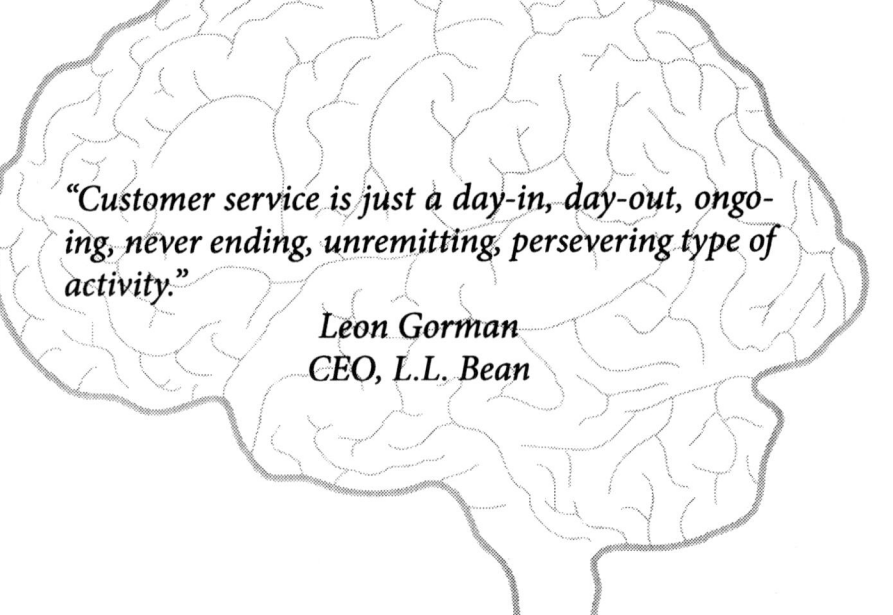

"Customer service is just a day-in, day-out, ongoing, never ending, unremitting, persevering type of activity."

Leon Gorman
CEO, L.L. Bean

COMMON SENSE MATTERS

On Selling

Keep Warm Program... *Keep the customer thinking of you*

A Keep Warm Program (KWP) is a campaign designed to create a continuous positive impression of you in the mind of your customer or prospect. It is an integral part of building a loyal customer/client base. We must first categorize our client base to effectively target our KWP. As we know, there are essentially two *types* of customer/client bases.

> ***Group A*** are buyers of large ticket items: a nonrecurring sale on a short- or medium-term basis. This market invariably is dominated by home sales, automobiles, possibly insurance, and similar type of products or services.
>
> ***Group B*** are *commodity* buyers: customers who deal with the vendor on a more frequent basis—weekly, monthly, or quarterly. Repeat business constitutes the bulk of this business and loyalty is the goal of the vendor.

There are four major categories for a KWP—which one you use depends on which one of the above categories your customer base falls into. Also know that you can "tailor make" the KWP for each individual customer.

Let us look at these four *categories* and discuss how to best use them:

I. **Contact Follow-up**
    For Group A customers, if the circumstance allows, an e-mail confirming your appointment is always a great first touch. Be sure to include all your contact information.

    When a salesperson is with a customer/prospect, there are always a slew of follow-up notes that should be made. This offers a great opportunity for REASONS TO RECONTACT THE CUSTOMER. It should be noted that very few Group A customers are closed after only one visit, and follow-up visits are usually the order of the day—whereas Group B customers can more often than not be closed when the product or service is being presented. <u>*Anything*</u> that is discussed during your presentation—an offer to give a quote, answer a query, inquire about a delivery, look into a comment about the industry—absolutely anything—this applies to both Group A and Group B customers—**MUST BE FOLLOWED UP WITH THE CUSTOMER/ PROSPECT.**

    Another nice initial follow up, which is a little more personal, is to send the customer a photograph that relates to something you discussed when you met with him. For example, you discover a mutual passion for fishing; take a photo on your next fishing trip of someone reeling in a catch and forward it to him with a brief comment like, "Hope you had the same luck this weekend as I did."

II. Subscriptions

This is a fantastic device for a KWP. Firstly, you act once, and the customer hears from you on a regular basis. Secondly, it is usually more personal than a business discussion and therefore helps build rapport.

In your discussions with your customer/prospect you obviously learn through your question-based selling technique what interests the customer has outside the business. They may be a health fanatic, or an avid hunter, possibly even a surfer. I had one customer that was fanatical about astronomy and science. The list goes on and on. Well, there are numerous magazines and publications that fit just about every interest. *Field & Stream Magazine* for the hunter; health and fitness publications for the health conscious; *The Surfer Magazine* for "you know who;" *Discover Magazine* for the science enthusiast, etc.

Subscription costs to you are minimal, and every month the customer/prospect gets a publication you sent them—which means they will be thinking of you every time they read it. If this isn't keeping them warm, then what is?

III. Industry Articles

Articles from industry specific publications are always great. And they are better than great if you personalize them. By that I mean, if there is an article in a newspaper or magazine that relates to your field, and you feel it may interest a customer, cut it out and in a pen write on the article something like, "Joe, thought this would interest you," with an arrow pointing to something specific. Then scan it and e-mail it to the customer. Another great touch! It shows you listen and care.

IV. E-Mails

This is old faithful. And it doesn't have to be an e-blast to every customer on your list. But regular e-mails can create loyalty and a positive sense of anticipation if they regularly feature:

- Specials
- Special offers
- Events of interest
- Clearance products
- New product introductions
- Even a cartoon (Dilbert works for some businesses)
- News bytes, etc.

A thoughtful, effective KWP program has the potential to warm up a cold prospect or turn a "warm" customer into a red-hot fan!

Every client you keep is one less you need to find.
Nigel Sanders
(Director, Cadbury Adams Confections)

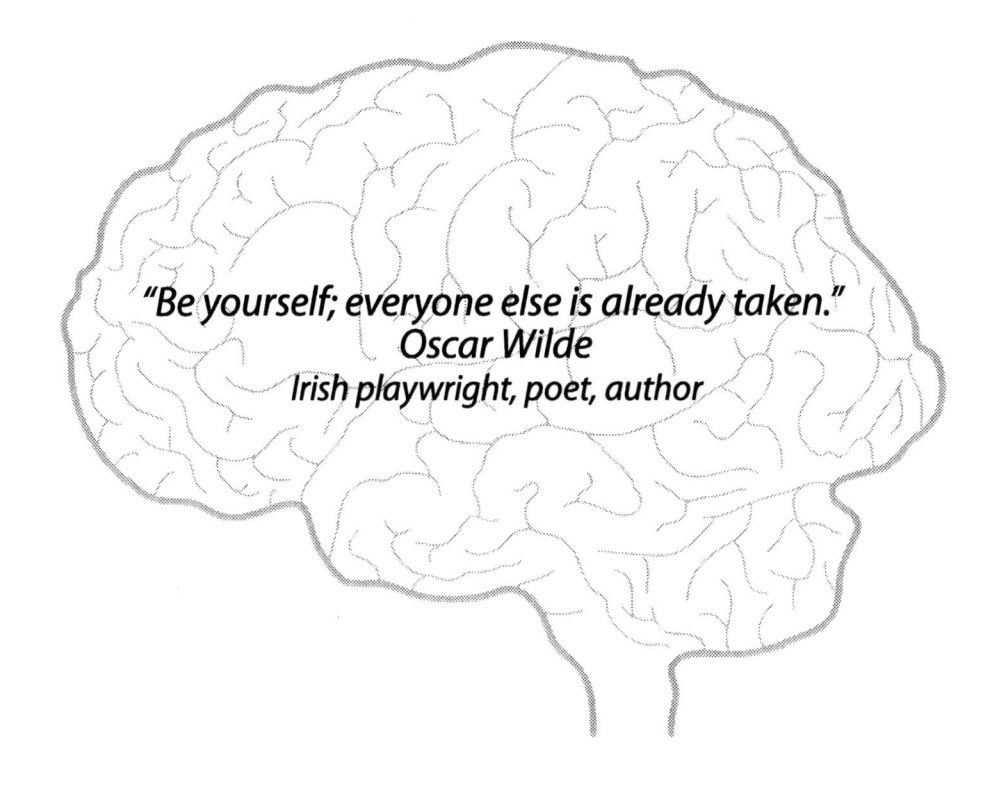

"Be yourself; everyone else is already taken."
Oscar Wilde
Irish playwright, poet, author

COMMON SENSE MATTERS

On Selling

*Be Memorable...*Don't be just a face in the crowd

We all want to be remembered in a positive way. We are in the profession of selling. So let's take a look at some effective ways to do that:

I. YOUR PHONE
- Change your voicemail every day. **"Hi, this is Eric, and today is Wednesday the fifteenth. I have a busy day today, but rest assured I will return your call by 4:00 p.m."...and DO it!**
- For years I did something very different and it was always commented on (an affirmation of *memorable*). The message was, **"Hi, this is Eric, and it's Tuesday the fourth. Leave your American Express number and the expiration date and I will get back to you."** People always commented how unusual the message was and it always got a chuckle. Memorable? You bet.

II. YOUR APPEARANCE
- Different industries are associated with different attire. Depending on the industry you are in, you may need to dress differently. Bankers and roofers dress differently. Make sure you dress in a way that will make your customer comfortable. **If you are selling farm equipment to a farmer, don't dress in a suit**! Always, however, be clean, neat, and well kempt.

- In the same vein, if your customer is soft-spoken, don't be a backslapping jokester. You will be remembered—but for the wrong reason. And remember to mirror your customers' body language.

III. YOUR IMMEDIATE FOLLOW-UP

The operative word here is *immediate*.

- Have Thank You cards (you can get them personalized at shutterfly.com), which you send to the customer *the same day*. Keep the stamped cards in your car, so all you need to do is write your messages and drop them in the mailbox. Imagine what an impact it will have on your customers if you mail the cards the same day you saw them, and they get them the next day!
- You should put your photograph on your business cards. Shutterfly.com will do this for you as well.
- Get your stamps from **stamps.com or Zazzle.com (or the good ol' United States Post Office).**
- You should have a laptop in your car. Can you imagine the impact you will have on your customer when **they receive an e-mail from you within thirty minutes of you leaving them, confirming your next *action item* for them??? If that does not make you memorable to them—then nothing will.**

You get only one chance to make a "first impression."
Make it a "lasting impression."